VERNACULAR HERMENEUTICS

edited by

R.S. Sugirtharajah

THE BIBLE AND POSTCOLONIALISM, 2

Series Editor:

R.S. Sugirtharajah

Sheffield
Academic Press

Published by
Sheffield Academic Press Ltd
Mansion House
19 Kingfield Road
Sheffield S11 9AS
England

Typeset by Sheffield Academic Press
and
Printed on acid-free paper in Great Britain
by Cromwell Press
Trowbridge, Wiltshire

British Library Cataloguing in Publication Data

A catalogue record for this book is available
from the British Library

ISBN 1-85075-943-X

Contents

Acknowledgments

As ever, a number of people have helped me in the production of this volume: my thanks to the contributors for all their efforts and full commitment to the project; Dan O'Connor for his advice and inspiration in all my research projects; Ralph Broadbent for his expertise in converting different software programmes into a single format; Meline Nielson, Griselda Lartey, Susan Abbot and Michael Gale, the staff of the Selly Oak Federation's Orchard Learning Centre, for their friendly and prompt service; The Drummond Trust, 3 Pitt Terrace, Stirling for their financial help; Jean Allen of the Sheffield Academic Press for her support and encouragement; Rebecca Cullen for her invaluable help and counsel in the production of this volume; and Sharada, my wife, for sharing in enthusiasm with me.

R.S. Sugirtharajah
Birmingham
England

Abbreviations

List of Contributors

David Tuesday Adamo, Delta State University, Abraka, Nigeria

Laura E. Donaldson, Women's Study Programme, The University of Iowa, Iowa City, USA

George Mulrain, United Theological College of the West Indies, Kingston, Jamaica

Dalila Nayap-Pot, a doctoral of ministry candidate at San Francisco Theological Seminary, San Anselmo, USA

R.S. Sugirtharajah, University of Birmingham, England

M. Thomas Thangaraj, Candler School of Theology, Atlanta, USA

Gerald O. West, School of Theology, University of Natal, Pietermaritzburg, South Africa

Vernacular Resurrections: An Introduction

R.S. SUGIRTHARAJAH

'Look', said Firoze, 'if you can sprinkle texts with fancy French terms, what's wrong with a little Sanskrit? Can't you see that it's a product of colonialism that prestige value is attached to one language rather than the other?' (Kirin Narayan, *Love, Stars and All That*).

At the risk of over generalizing, Third World biblical hermeneutics falls into two categories—liberation-focused and culture-sensitive. While the former privileges liberation as a crucial hermeneutical key, the latter mobilizes indigenous cultural nuances for theological enterprises. I should make it clear that these are not neatly demarcated entities, but that they often interact and are mutually dependent. The most popular and most accessible to Western audiences is the liberation-focussed Latin American liberation theology. To this one could add South African liberation theology, which owes its initial popularity to the Kairos document (British Council of Churches: 1986). Recently, there has been an explosion of interest in Korean minjung, Indian dalit, Japanese burakumin, and the indigenous peoples' theologies. Women interpreters have also brought to light the existence of feminist hermeneutics in non-Western cultures. In spite of the adversarial and partisan nature of these theologies, their popularity in Western circles in general, and in scholarly guilds in particular, is because of their shared assumptions with the metropolitan academic culture. The intellectual structure of these theologies, the way they mobilize the grand theorists of Western disciplines, the overly Christocentric framework they advocate, the modernist assumptions they deploy, the theoretical tools they summon,

make them easy targets for Western absorption, even colonization. While espousing and retaining grass-roots interests, the
theologies of Gutierrez, Boff and Sobrino fall largely within the
Western academic syntax, which makes them easy to incorporate.
Kosuke Koyama's observation on the Kairos document is an apt
one here. He says that the content and the method are so
thoroughly Western that as a result the document is better known
to Germans than to Zulus (Koyama 1993: 101).

The dominant presence of liberation theology has tended to
overshadow and conceal context-sensitive vernacular texts, and
has also silenced the pioneering and often daring efforts of an
earlier generation of theologians. This volume is one of the few to
rectify the situation (see also Smith-Christopher 1995). The vernacular hermeneutics which privileges indigenous culture as an
authentic site for doing theology, and which focuses on native
characteristics and ideas, does not rank as highly as liberation
theologies, which are able to straddle different cultures. The
interpretations included here are context-sensitive and are concerned with, and draw heavily on, particular language traditions
or cultural insights; they are bound by their own rules. Despite
the stranglehold of Western interpretation, and its claim to uni-
versality, vernacular hermeneutics is postmodern in its eagerness
to celebrate the local, and postcolonial in its ability to disturb and
dislodge the reigning imported theories. Vernacular reading is
often undertaken by the indigenes themselves. These interpretative practices are hardly heard of in Western academies because
such practices seek to acquire and celebrate their identity by delv-
ing into their indigenous resources. They naturally reject the
superintending tendencies of Western intellectual tradition.
Hence the theological reflections of a Vedanayagam or a Krishna
Pillai or a Vaman Tilak are relatively unknown. (Though I mention only Indian names, there are comparable figures in other
cultures who have engaged in similar hermeneutical enterprises.)
Even when they are available in translations, they are deemed not
to be addressing the weightier theological issues and are dis-
missed as devotional effusions or spiritual lamentations. The non-
receptivity to and unpopularity of these theologies in Western
circles is not due to the fact they are done in vernacular languages
or are not translatable or are incomprehensible or unmarketable,

but is because they employ a set of ground rules which is different from the protocol set by the academy. They address issues closer to home. H.Y. Sharada Prasad's observation about Indian responses to the writings of Indians in English and the writings of Indians in the vernacular is equally true of Third World biblical hermeneutics. The response to Anglo-Indian writing will be to say 'how interesting', whereas the response to fiction written in regional languages will be 'how true and so much nearer home' (quoted in Nayar 1998: 23). Vernacular hermeneutics is about being nearer home and getting closer to the roots.

In Practice and Theory

What this collection aims to do is to make visible the spectacular ways in which the vernacular has been creatively and critically incorporated into current interpretative practices. The essays in this volume are grouped into two categories, but these categories are fluid and the essays could be easily accommodated in either one. The first section, 'Indigenizing the Narratives', deals with exegetical reworkings which are informed by vernacular heritage and by the indigene's own identity. Laura Donaldson looks again at the book of Ruth and undertakes a fascinating rereading as a Cherokee woman. She tries to reposition Ruth in the light of the specific cultural and historical predicament of American Indian women. In doing so, she dismantles the dominant readings which have made Ruth a paradigmatic convert/assimilator. In the process, she recovers another often written-out and under-exegeted indigene character in the text—Orpah, the sister-in-law of Ruth, who returned to her mother's house. Donaldson's contention is that it is Orpah who connotes hope and provides emancipatory vision for the Cherokee woman because it was she who embraced her own clan and cultural traditions. Read from Orpah's point of view, we see a different Ruth. In his paper, Gerald West defines vernacular hermeneutics as the reading strategy, using their own resources, of ordinary indigenous readers of the Bible, mainly the marginalized, who bring their own critical consciousness to the text. For him, vernacular is not an interesting reading but an interested reading which always sides with the marginalized. Using the South African artist Azariah Mbatha's woodcut drawing of the Joseph story as a hermeneutical launching pad, West recovers African aspects of the story and relocates the Bible in Africa, where most of the story takes place. He also problematizes the role of the informed reader in representing the subalterns. In the next essay, Dalila Nayap-Pot, unlike Donaldson, elects to resituate herself within the narrative world of Naomi and Ruth. She does so in order to make sense of her own subjectivity and also in an effort to control the situation in which she is placed as an expatriate in an alien context. In other words, she disconnects the narrative from its historical and cultural context and appropriates these biblical characters to address her own, related predicament. The biblical characters, Ruth and Naomi, become a vehicle for asserting her own identity and reality. The last essay in this section is an illustration of how the Bible, which was used as a weapon of suppression of indigenous cultures, is now being turned around by the indigenous people themselves as a weapon of defence and a weapon to cherish. David Adamo looks at the book of Psalms, so often quoted in Africa, and demonstrates how, unlike Western readers who approach it with assumptions dominated by modernist and rationalist values, Africans find the Psalms helpful during times of pain, joy, confusion and danger. More importantly, what the essay demonstrates is how the indigenes mobilize their own cultural values to open up the text.

Part II, 'Reinstating the Local', contains three articles. The first one (mine) tries to provide a definition of vernacular hermeneutics, and illustrates it with examples selected from different cultural contexts. It concludes that, while celebrating the arrival of the vernacular, one needs to be aware that the vernacular itself can become a conservative tool when it is used to emphasize purity over against plurality and diversity. George Mulrain argues for a Caribbean interpretative practice, which, though it stands within the tradition of black hermeneutics, has to chalk out its own identity. He advocates the priority of the reader, particularly the Church reader, and at the same time he wants to protect the integrity of the text. In the last essay, M. Thomas Thangaraj investigates how the Tamils in South India initially appropriated the Hindu term Veda (Scripture) to denote the Christian Bible. Prompted partially by the missionaries, and partially by their ignorance of and the inaccessibility of the Vedas, they began to view them negatively. However, a minority among them—both missionaries and local Christians—came to see the Vedas as a *preparatio evangelii* and as taking the place of the Hebrew Scriptures for Indian Christians. Now, in a changed hermeneutical context, Thangaraj points out that the Tamils have moved on from calling the Bible 'Veda', partly because of the urge to desanskritize, but also to respect the integrity of the Hindu religious text and, more importantly, to recognize the multi-scriptural context of biblical hermeneutics.

A Cautious Advocacy

Despite the wide range of positions these essays embody and advocate, they share certain common insights—the indigenous context as the source of cultural value and meaning; the indigenous heritage as the vantage point for a critical understanding of contemporary forms of imperialism; and Western representations of cultural otherness as reinforcements for various colonial projects.

At a time when the world is ever shrinking and being linked by transnational capital and multinational corporations, when the globe is celebrated as a village where everyone is interconnected, and when the idea of a stable home is an elusive concept, looking for a native or a vernacular heritage may be a futile or even a utopian endeavour. In such circumstances, it is not always easy to identify an authentic indigenous person. One of the tests prescribed in the Hebrew Scriptures—using vernacular as a way of ascertaining identity—may not be appropriate today. The book of Judges describes how the men of Gilead, under the leadership of Jephthah, unmasked the Ephraimite infiltrators crossing the river Jordan by asking them to pronounce the word for 'running stream', *shibboleth*. If the infiltrators said '*sibboleth*', their dialect exposed them as fugitives from Ephraim, and the text reports that 42,000 Ephraimites were slain (Judg. 12). At a time when vernacular cultures and languages are intermingled with those of the metropolis, it is not always feasible to use dialect as a test of identity. In our enthusiasm to recover the native, we may put ourselves in the double predicament of finding redeeming values both in the indigene and in the text. Both have to be approached cautiously. By eulogizing the ascendancy of the native and revalorizing the text, we may end up by fixing, absolutizing and immobilizing both. We may finish up advocating and reaffirming the 'cosy indigene', and endowing the text with unwarranted numinous and magical properties. In our desire to resurrect the real native, it is worthwhile heeding Rey Chow's warning—not to sanctify the image of the native or to regard the native as the site of genuine knowledge. She goes on to say that 'our fascination with the native, the oppressed, the savage, and all such figures is therefore a desire to hold on to an unchanging certainty somewhere outside our own "fake experience"' (1993: 53). In projecting an idealized native, we may be culpable of fabricating our own version of 'orientalism' and of partaking in myth making.

Finally, for most of the essayists, for a variety of reasons, the academy has become their natural home. As long as we are part of it, we, too, are tainted and none of us would claim to be the original indigene—if ever such a species existed. Some of us may be puzzled by some of our own heritage of cultural customs and native practices, even embarrassed by them. We may not ideally be able to represent the indigenes. But we can engage in what we are supposed to be good at doing. We can still be their spokespersons and write about what we know of them, so that indigenes (whether they be Aborigines or Native Americans, Dalits or Adivasis) and their conditions may be better known, and their memories kept alive. By so doing, we can offer counter information and check the negative and stereotypical images emanating from powerful and authoritative sources. This volume is a modest attempt to keep the memory alive while at the same time being wary of promulgating distorted memories. I end with a conversation in A. Sivanadan's *When Memory Dies*, a novel set in Sri Lanka. It takes place against the backdrop of the ethnic conflict in the island, when both Singhalese and Tamils manufacture memories to assert their identity and superiority. The conversation in a way sums up the design and mood of this volume:

> 'When memories die a people die'
> 'What if we make up false memories'
> 'That's worse, that's murder' (Sivanadan 1997: 335).

BIBLIOGRAPHY

British Counil of Churches
    1986   *The Kairos Document: A Theological Comment on the Political Crisis in South Africa* (London: Catholic Institute for International Relations and British Council of Churches, 2nd rev. edn; Broamfontein: Skotaville).

Chow, Rey
    1993   *Writing Diaspora: Tactics of Interpretation in Contemporary Cultural Studies* (Bloomington: Indiana University Press).

Koyama, Kosuke
    1993   'Theological Education: Its Unities and Diversities', *Theological Education Supplement* 30: 87-105

Kirin, Narayan
    1994   *Love, Stars and All That* (New Delhi: Penguin Books).

Nayar, Radhakrishnan
    1998   'Vernacular Spectacular', *The Times Higher Education Supplement*, 6 February 1998: 23.

Sivanadan, A.
    1997   *When Memory Dies* (London: Arcadia Books).

Smith-Christopher, Daniel
    1995   *Text and Experience: Towards A Cultural Exegesis of the Bible* (Sheffield: Sheffield Academic Press).

Part I

INDIGENIZING THE NARRATIVES

THE SIGN OF ORPAH:
READING RUTH THROUGH NATIVE EYES

LAURA E. DONALDSON

Prologue: Reading in the Contact Zone

This was no party
how the house was shaking.
They were trying
to nibble my bones, gnaw
my tribal tongue.
They took turns
pretending they had the power
to disembowel my soul
and force me to give them
my face to wear
for Halloween.
They like to play
that I want to change,
that I don't mind ending myself
in their holy book.
They think they can just twist till the blood has drained
and I am as white
and delightsome
as can be.

(Wendy Rose, 'The Mormons Next Door')[1]

The act of reading the Bible has been fraught with difficulty and contradiction for indigenous peoples. On the one hand, the translation of God's Book into Native vernacular comes with a high price: the forcing of oral tongues into static alphabets and its

---

1. In Wendy Rose, *Going to War with All my Relations: New and Selected Poems* (Flagstaff, AZ: Entrada Books, 1993).

context of a colonizing Christianity. All too often, biblical reading has produced traumatic disruptions within Native societies and facilitated what we now call culturecide. On the other hand, this depressingly long history of victimization should not obscure the ways in which Native peoples have actively resisted deracinating processes by reading the Bible on their own terms.[2] As Rigoberta Menchú (Quiché Mayan) notes in her moving *testimonio, I, Rigoberta Menchú*:

> We accept these Biblical forefathers as if they were our own ances-
> tors, while still keeping within our own culture and our own cus-
> toms... For instance the Bible tells us that there were kings who
> beat Christ. We drew a parallel with our king, Tecún Umán, who
> was defeated and persecuted by the Spaniards, and we take that as
> our own reality.[3]

Whether Menchú and the Quiché Mayan people scan a printed page or learn the stories by heart, they claim the Bible's 'reality' as their own and thus exceed the bounds of imperial exegesis. A vivid example of this dynamic emerges from the way Menchú and other women of her community learned to negotiate the biblical narratives of liberation.

As Menchú remarks, the Quiché began their reading process by searching the scripture for stories representing 'each one of us'. While the men of Chimel village adopted Moses and the Exodus as their paradigm text of liberation, the women preferred the tale of Judith, who 'fought very hard for her people and made many attacks against the king they had then, until she finally had his head'.[4] Here, the distinct hermeneutic tradition of Mayan women begins to emerge—one that does not indoctrinate the reader with the colonizer's values but, rather, helps them understand and respond to their own historical situation (in this case, the brutal war being waged against them by the Guatemalan regime of García Lucas). Menchú rejects the belief that the Bible, or the tale of Judith and Holofernes, themselves effect change: 'It's more that each one of us learns to understand his reality and wants to

2. 'Deracination' comes from the Latin word meaning 'to uproot or to alienate'.

3. Rigoberta Menchú, *I, Rigoberta Menchú: An Indian Woman in Guatemala* (ed. E. Burgos-Debray; trans. A. Wright; London: Verso, 1984), p. 80.

4. Menchú, *I, Rigoberta Menchú*, p. 131.

devote himself to others. More than anything else, it was a form of learning for us.'[5] Through this statement, she articulates a process of reading practiced by many of the world's Native peoples—a process that actively selects and invents, rather than passively accepts, from the literate materials exported to them by the dominant Euro-Spanish culture. For Menchú, this transculturation of meaning emerges from the act of biblical reading in the contact zone.

In her book *Imperial Eyes: Travel Writing and Transculturation,* Mary Louise Pratt defines a contact zone as the space of colonial encounters where people who are divided both geographically and historically come into contact with each other and establish ongoing relations, usually involving conditions of severe inequality and intractable conflict.[6] She coins this term, instead of borrowing the more Eurocentric 'colonial frontier', because she wants 'to foreground the interactive, improvisational dimensions of colonial encounters so easily ignored or suppressed by diffusionist accounts of conquest and domination'.[7] For Pratt, a 'contact' perspective treats the bonds among colonizers and colonized (for example, Quiché and *Ladinos*) as implying co-presence, mutual influence and interlocking understandings that emerge from deep asymmetries of power. In this essay I will read the biblical book of Ruth through just such a contact perspective forged by the interaction of biblical narrative, the realities of Anglo-European imperialism and the traditions of Cherokee women. This rereading is marked not only by the colonial history of Indian–white relations but also by the persistence of American Indian traditions; not only by Anglo-European genocide but also by Native 'survivance';[8] not only by subjugation but also by resistance.

Scholars have traditionally regarded the book of Ruth as one of the Hebrew Bible's literary jewels: 'a brief moment of serenity in

5.   Menchú, *I, Rigoberta Menchú,* p. 135.

6.   Mary Louise Pratt, *Imperial Eyes: Travel Writing and Transculturation* (London: Routledge, 1992), p. 6.

7.   Pratt, *Imperial Eyes,* p. 7.

8.   The term 'survivance' is used by Gerald Vizenor (Chippewa) to describe the complicated gestures of Native survival in the contact zone of contemporary American culture.

the stormy world'.[9] According to Herman Gunkel, for example, Ruth represents one of those 'glorious *poetical narratives'* that exhibits 'a widow's love lasting beyond death and the grave'.[10] Feminist biblical critics have persuasively challenged this view by exposing its masculinist and heterosexist bias. For these interpreters, Ruth's love embodies the love of a woman-identified woman who is forced into the patriarchal institution of levirate marriage in order to survive. It is here—with this struggle over the meaning of women in the text—that I wish to begin my own articulation of the difficult and often dangerous terrain charted by the contact zone. Like Menchú, I hope that my reading of Ruth will function as a form of learning that will enable Native people both to understand more thoroughly how biblical interpretation has impacted us, and to assert our own perspectives more strongly. It seems fitting, then, that this journey begin with a crisis: the journey of Naomi and her husband Elimelech into Moab, the scandalous country of Lot's daughters.

The Daughters of Lot

Thus both daughters of Lot became pregnant by their father. The firstborn bore a son, and named him Moab; he is the ancestor of the Moabites to this day (Gen. 19.36-37, NRSV).

While Israel was staying at Shittim, the people began to have sexual relations with the women of Moab. These invited the people to the sacrifices of their gods, and the people ate and bowed down to their gods. Thus Israel yoked itself to the Baal of Peor, and the Lord's anger was kindled against Israel (Num. 25.1-3, NRSV).

There was a famine in the house of bread—the literal meaning of the name 'Bethlehem'—and only the threat of starvation motivated Elimelech, a god-fearing Israelite, to forsake his home for the country harboring the sexually promiscuous and scandalous Moabites. Even worse, once he and his family arrive there, their two sons defy the Hebrew proscription against foreign marriage

---

9. Danna Nolan Fewell and David M. Gunn, *Compromising Redemption: Relating Characters in the Book of Ruth* (Louisville, KY: Westminster/John Knox Press, 1990), p. 11.

10. H. Gunkel, *What Remains of the Old Testament, and Other Essays* (trans. A.K. Dallas; New York: Macmillan, 1928), p. 21.

by taking the Moabite women Orpah and Ruth as wives. Indeed, for centuries the Israelites had reviled this people as degenerate and, particularly, regarded Moabite women as the agents of impurity and evil. Even the name 'Moab' exhibits this contempt, since it allegedly originates in the incestuous liaison between Lot and his daughters. According to the biblical narrative in Genesis 19, Lot's daughters devise a plan to get him drunk on succeeding nights so that they can seduce him. Both women become pregnant through this relationship and both have sons. Lot's eldest daughter openly declares her son's origins when she calls him Moab, or 'from my father'. We glimpse the result of their actions in Deuteronomy which declares that, even to the tenth generation, 'no Ammonite or Moabite shall be admitted to the assembly of the Lord' (Deut. 23.3).

As Randall Bailey notes in his fascinating essay on sex and sexuality in Hebrew canon narratives,

> the effect of both the narrative in Genesis 19 and the laws
> in Deuteronomy 23…is to label within the consciousness of the
> reader the view of these nations as nothing more than 'incestuous
> bastards'. Through the use of repetition in the narrative in
> Genesis 19…the narrator grinds home the notion of *mamzērîm*
> [bastards].[11]

Further, according to Bailey, this dehumanization through graphic sexual innuendo enables one to read other parts of the Deuteronomic history—David's mass slaughter of the Moabites in 2 Sam. 8.2 or the ritual humiliation of the Ammonites in 2 Sam. 12.26-31—as warranted and even meritorious.[12]

The belief in Moabite women as a hypersexualized threat to Israelite men prophetically augurs the Christian attitude toward the indigenous women of the Americas. Indeed, as early as 1511, an anonymous Dutch pamphleteer vouched that 'these folke lyven lyke bestes without any reasonablenes… And the wymen be

---

11. Randall Bailey, 'They're Nothing but Incestuous Bastards: The Polemical Use of Sex and Sexuality in Hebrew Canon Narratives', in Fernando F. Segovia and Mary Ann Tolbert (eds.), *Reading from This Place*. I. *Social Location and Biblical Interpretation in the United States* (Philadelphia: Fortress Press, 1995), pp. 121-38 (131).

12. Bailey, 'They're Nothing', p. 132.

very hoote and dysposed to lecherdnes.'[13] Significantly (and, I would add, symptomatically), no less a personage than Thomas Jefferson, the second President of the United States and a framer of its Constitution, forges an important link between the Israelite attitude toward the Moabites and the Christian attitude toward American Indians in his own discourse on the book of Ruth. After finishing his *Notes on the State of Virginia* (1787)[14]—one of the most important influences upon Euramerican attitudes toward Native peoples—Jefferson submitted the manuscript for comments to Charles Thomson, then Secretary of Congress. Thomson's remarks were included in the published version because, as Jefferson enthused, 'the following observations...have too much merit not to be communicated'. In his response to the section that describes the nation's 'Aborigines', Thomson observes that an alleged lack of 'ardor' in Indian men most probably originated in the forwardness of their women:

> Instances similar to that of Ruth and Boaz are not uncommon among them. For though the women are modest and diffident, and so bashful that they seldom lift up their eyes, and scarce ever look a man full in the face, yet being brought up on great subjection, custom and manners reconcile them to modes of acting, which, judged of by Europeans, would be deemed inconsistent with the rules of female decorum and propriety.[15]

Jefferson endorses Thomson's remarks by locating the relevant biblical passage: 'When Boaz had eaten and drank, and his heart was merry, he went to lie down at the end of the heap of corn: and Ruth came softly, and uncovered his feet, and laid her down. Ruth iii.7'.[16] Although cloaked in the rhetoric of Enlightenment gentility, the statements by Thomson and Jefferson nevertheless

13. As cited in Robert F. Berkhofer, Jr, *The White Man's Indian: Images of the American Indian from Columbus to the Present* (New York: Random House, 1978), p. 10.

14. T. Jefferson, *Notes on the State of Virginia* (ed. William Peden; New York: W.W. Norton, 1982).

15. Jefferson, *Notes*, p. 201.

16. Jefferson, *Notes*, p. 297. Since in Hebrew 'feet' is often used as a euphemism for a man's genitals, Ruth is clearly initiating some sort of sexual encounter with Boaz.

disseminate a cautionary tale that is quite similar to the one con-
cerning the Moabites: both American Indian and Moabite women
exist as agents not only of evil and impurity but also of men's
sexual frigidity. Given such negative representations, we need to
investigate why the biblical author of Ruth chooses to foreground
precisely this ideological nexus by consistently identifying the pro-
tagonist as 'Ruth of Moab'.

Ruth 2.6 provides an insightful glimpse into this process. After
Elimelech and his two sons die, Naomi and Ruth return to Bethlehem. Naomi subsequently, and recklessly according to some
critics, sends her daughter-in-law into the fields of Boaz, a relative
of her late husband, who notices the young widow and asks his
servant to whom she belongs. 'The servant who was in charge of
the reapers answered, "she is the Moabite who came back with
Naomi from the country of Moab".' The redundant doubling of
ethnic markers in this passage—the Moabite from the country of
Moab—emphasizes the text's construction of Ruth not only as a
gērāh, or resident alien, but also as an alien who comes from a
despised and barbaric country. However, the significance of this
particular repetition has been construed in widely variant ways.

For example, the rabbis who wrote *Ruth R.* believe that it rein-
forces Ruth's role as a paradigmatic convert to Judaism who
'turned her back upon wicked Moab and its worthless idols to
become a God-fearing Jewess—loyal daughter-in-law, modest
bride, renowned ancestress of Israel's great King David'.[17] The
Iggereth Shmuel expands this view and suggests that the quality of
Ruth's faith even surpasses that of Abraham since, unlike Ruth, he
only left home after God commanded him to do so.[18] For more
contemporary critics the message of Ruth's identity is not one of
conversion, but rather of 'interethnic bonding' that parallels the
gender bond established when Naomi's daughter-in-law 'clings' to
her husband's mother instead of returning home.[19] William

17. Kathryn Pfisterer Darr, *Far More Precious than Jewels: Perspectives on
Biblical Women* (Louisville, KY: Westminster/John Knox Press, 1991), p. 72.

18. Darr, *Far More Precious*, p. 72.

19. The verb 'to cling' is particularly revealing here, since its customary
usage involves the relationships of husbands to wives and of humans to
Yahweh. Both womanist and feminist critics have used this linguistic turn to
argue for Ruth's status as a woman-identified woman. Or, a woman who

Phipps articulates this position when he argues that the repetition of 'Ruth the Moabite' connotes 'vital religion and ethics in a time of bigotry and mayhem',[20] and acts as an antidote to the xenophobia of the postexilic Jewish community. Rather than rejection of the Moabites and acceptance of the Israelites, then, Ruth's story conjures a vision of ethnic and cultural harmony through the house of David, which claims her as a direct ancestress.

While the presentation of Ruth as a character manifesting the virtues of tolerance and multiculturalism is appealing, Robert Maldonado's attempt to develop a *malinchista* hermeneutics[21] complicates this view by exposing its political and historical ambiguities. For Maldonado, a theologian of Mexican and Hungarian descent, the biblical figure of Ruth foreshadows the existence of *La Malinche,* or Doña Marina, the Aztec woman who became a consort of, and collaborator with, the conquistador Hernán Cortés. *La Malinche*'s legacy endures not only in historical Mexican consciousness but also in its linguistic vernacular: '*Malinchista* is a common term for a person who adopts foreign values, assimilates to foreign cultures, or serves foreign interests... The usage ties the meaning of betrayal in Mexican Spanish to the history of colonialism and Indian White relations...'[22] Yet *La Malinche* harbors deeper and even more personal levels of betrayal, since she was sold as a young girl to some Mayan traders—an experience that generated the bilingualism so crucial to her equivocal status. After she had been acquired by Cortés she was 'given' to one of his officers and subsequently married to another conquistador. We begin to glimpse at least some of the complex and disturbing elements underpinning *La Malinche*'s collaboration

---

embodied the capacity 'to care passionately about the quality of another woman's life, to respect each other's choices, and to allow for each other's differences' (Renita Weems, *Just a Sister Away: A Womanist Vision of Women's Relationships in the Bible* [San Diego: Lura Media, 1988], p. 34).

20. William E. Phipps, *Assertive Biblical Women* (Contributions in Women's Studies, 128; Westport, CT: Greenwood Press, 1992), p. 67.

21. R. Maldonado, 'Reading Malinche Reading Ruth: Toward a Hermeneutics of Betrayal', *Semeia* 72 (1995), pp. 91-109.

22. Mary Louise Pratt, '"Yo soy la malinche": Chicana Writers and the Poetics of Ethnonationalism', *Callaloo* 16 (1993), pp. 859-73 (860); as cited in Maldonado, 'Reading Malinche', p. 99.

with her colonizers. The similarities between the story of Doña Marina and the actions of Ruth lead Maldonado provocatively to ask: 'Could Ruth be a Moabite Malinche'?[23] Maldonado answers his own question with a strong 'maybe'—precisely because of the redundant identification of Ruth described above, as well as his own investment in *mestizaje,* or the resistant discourse of racial and cultural mixing.

American Indians have a much more suspicious attitude toward the privileging of mixedness, be it *mestizaje, métissage* or life in the borderlands. After all, 'mixing' is precisely what Thomas Jefferson proposed as the final solution to the seemingly irresolvable 'Indian problem'. To a visiting delegation of Wyandots, Chippewas and Shawnees he confidently predicted that 'in time, you will be as we are; you will become one people with us. Your blood will mix with ours; and will spread, with ours, over this great island.'[24] And what better way to accomplish this commingling than with the paradigm of intermarriage that we glimpse in the book of Ruth? Indeed, one could argue that this 'moment of serenity in the stormy world of the Hebrew Bible' exists as the prototype for both the vision of Thomas Jefferson and all those who facilitated conquest of indigenous peoples through the promotion of assimilation.

This social absorption prophetically evokes the fate of many American Indian women and children. In the historically matrilineal Cherokee culture, for example, Jefferson's vision of 'mingling' and the realities of intermarriage wreaked havoc upon tribal organization and development. Wives now went to live with their white husbands—a practice that was contrary to the ancient custom of husbands residing in their wives' domicile. Further, according to Wilma Mankiller (the former Principal Chief of the Cherokee Nation), the children of these relationships assumed their fathers' surnames and became heirs to their father's, rather than their mother's, houses and possessions.[25] Intermarriage

23. Maldonado, 'Reading Malinche', p. 101.

24. T. Jefferson, *The Writings of Thomas Jefferson* (ed. A.E. Bergh; Washington, DC: Thomas Jefferson Memorial Association of the United States, 1907), p. 464.

25. Wilma Mankiller with Michael Wallis, *Mankiller: A Chief and her People* (New York: St Martin's Press, 1984), p. 26.

between whites and Indians severely disrupted the traditions of Cherokee women, since a genealogy that had for time immemorial passed from mother to son or daughter now shifted to the father and drastically curtailed women's power. In contrast to Maldonado, I would argue that the book of Ruth similarly foregrounds the use of intermarriage as an assimilationist strategy.

Soon after Ruth marries Boaz, the text states that she conceives and bears a son.

> Then Naomi took the child and laid him in her bosom, and became his nurse. The women of the neighborhood gave him a name saying, 'A son has been born to Naomi'. They named him Obed; he became the father of Jesse, the father of David (4.13-17).

As Danna Nolan Fewell and David Gunn note, through this announcement Ruth effectively disappears into the household of Boaz, and the legacy of the future king David closes the door upon her story.[26] In other words—although Fewell and Gunn do not use these terms—Ruth's assimilation becomes complete through Obed's transfer to Naomi, the proper Jewish woman, and to Boaz, the Israelite husband. The issue then becomes, What motivates this effacement and what ideological ends does it fulfill?

Even to begin answering this question, however, we must first understand how Ruth is linked to two seemingly disparate female icons—one from the Hebrew Bible and the other from the annals of American Indian history: Raḥab and Pocahontas. Both of these women have played important roles in the construction of national narratives and both, like *La Malinche*, have been mythologized as facilitating conquest through their relationships with colonizing men.

The Anti-Pocahontas Perplex

You made a decision. My place is with you. I go where you go.
(Stands With A fist to John Dunbar in *Dances with Wolves*)

Raḥab, of course, is Ruth's other mother-in-law and the Canaanite prostitute who gave birth to Boaz (see Mt. 1.5). The events leading to this remarkable transformation of status are memorialized in the book of Joshua, ch. 2, and can be briefly summarized as

---

26. Fewell and Gunn, *Compromising Redemption*, p. 105.

follows. Joshua, who was leading the Israelite invasion of Canaan, sends two spies to reconnoiter the city of Jericho. These two men 'entered the house of a prostitute whose name was Raḥab and spent the night there' (2.1). When the king of Jericho hears of the spies' presence, he orders Raḥab to surrender them. She refuses and hides them under stalks of flax that she had laid out on the roof. After nightfall she visits the men and requests that, since she has dealt kindly with them, they might in turn spare her and her family 'and deliver our lives from death'. Jericho does indeed fall: 'But Raḥab the prostitute, with her family and all who belonged to her, Joshua spared. Her family has lived in Israel ever since' (Josh. 6.25). Further, she is extolled in the Greek Bible as a paragon of faith and granted a high status as the ancestress of David and Jesus. Like her daughter-in-law Ruth, Raḥab embodies a foreign woman, a Canaanite Other who crosses over from paganism to monotheism and is rewarded for this act by absorption into the genealogy of her husband and son—in this case, into the house of Salmon and, ultimately, of David. And, like Ruth, she represents the position of the indigene in the text, or of those people who occupied the promised land before the invasion of the Israelites.

However, the narrative figures of Raḥab and Ruth conjure not only the position of the indigene in the biblical text but also the specific cultural and historical predicament of American Indian women. Cherokee scholar Rayna Green has identified this predicament as 'the Pocahontas Perplex'—one of Euramerica's most important master narratives about Native women. It is named for the daughter of Powhatan and the mythology that has arisen around one of the most culturally significant encounters between Indians and whites. In this version of the story Powhatan Indians capture Captain John Smith and his men while they are exploring the territory around what is now called Jamestown, Virginia. After marching Smith to their town, the Indians lay his head on a large stone and prepare to kill him with their clubs. Precisely at that moment, Pocahontas—the favorite daughter of Powhatan—uses her body as a human shield and prevents Smith from being executed. She then further intercedes on behalf of the English colonists, who were starving after a long winter, and consequently saves not only the colonists but also the future of English colonization.[27]

As a master narrative with an ideological function, the Pocahontas Perplex construes the nobility of Pocahontas and other Indian women as 'princess' who

> 'must save or give aid to white men'. As Green notes, 'the only good Indian—male or female, Squanto, Pocahontas, Sacagawea, Cochise, the Little Mohee or the Indian Doctor—rescues and helps white men'. But the Indian woman is even more burdened by this narrow definition of a 'good Indian', for it is she, not the males, whom white men desire sexually.[28]

A consequence of this desire is that the 'good' feminine image also implies the 'bad' one. She is the Squaw whose degraded sexuality is vividly summarized in the frontier song 'Little Red Wing': She 'lays on her back in a cowboy shack, and lets cowboys poke her in the crack'.[29] The specter of the Squaw—also known as a daughter of Lot—retroactively taints Raḥab and Ruth; after all,

27. While most Americans still believe in the myth that Pocahontas loved John Smith, a growing body of scholarship has significantly revised this tale of their encounter. Rayna Green and Kathleen Brown are among those who have persuasively argued that Smith's own account of his captivity, near-execution and rescue by Pocahontas eloquently testifies to yet another example of misrecognized and misinterpreted cultural difference. Brown, for example, contends that Smith's recording of Pocahontas covering his body with her own was most probably part of an adoption ritual in which Powhatan defined his relationship to him as one of patriarchal dominance ('The Anglo-Algonquian Gender Frontier', in Nancy Shoemaker [ed.], *Negotiators of Change: Historical Perspectives on American Indian Women* [London: Routledge, 1995], pp. 26-48 [39]). Unfortunately, 'Smith understood neither the ritual adoption taking place nor the significance of Powhatan's promise to make him a werowance and to "for ever esteeme him as [he did] his son Nantaquoud"' (p. 40). Green (in 'The Pocahontas Perplex: The Image of Indian Women in American Culture', *Massachusetts Review* [autumn 1975], pp. 698-714) provides a further gloss. She notes that, as the daughter of the tribe's leader and a woman of considerable status, Pocahontas served as Smith's 'mother', for he had to be reborn, after a symbolic death, as one of the tribe. Thus, Pocahontas was not delaying Smith's execution and thwarting her own people when she threw her body over his. She was in fact acting on behalf of her people (p. 35).

28. Green, 'The Pocahontas Perplex', p. 703.

29. Green, 'The Pocahontas Perplex', p. 711.

the former earns her living as a prostitute and, according to Thomas Jefferson and company, the latter's behavior in the biblical counterpart of the cowboy shack was shockingly immoral. Such a debased starting point enables the scriptural stories to proclaim even more stridently the metamorphosis of Raḥab and Ruth into the Israelite version of the Pocahontas Perplex. In this scenario, Salmon and Boaz stand in for John Smith. The result, however, remains the same. An indigenous woman forsakes her people and aligns herself with the men whom Yahweh had directed to 'break down their altars, smash their pillars, burn their Asherah poles with fires, and hew down the idols of their gods, and thus blot out their name from their places' (Deut. 12.3).

From an American-Indian perspective, then, the midrashic interpretation of Ruth as the paradigmatic convert who 'turned her back upon wicked Moab and its worthless idols to become a God-fearing Jewess'[30] seems a much more accurate description of the text's actual function than Robert Maldonado's appeal to some undecidable state of *mestizaje*. Indeed, even Ruth's name affirms the hermeneutic acumen of the rabbis, since it derives from the Hebrew root *rwh*, meaning 'watering to saturation'.[31] However, whereas the success of this ideological irrigation inspires rejoicing on behalf of the Israelites, it is an instance of mourning for American Indian women. Yet another relative has succumbed to—been filled up by and 'saturated' by—a hegemonic culture.

Is there no hope in the book of Ruth? Is it nothing but a tale of conversion/assimilation and the inevitable vanishing of the indigene in the literary and social text? In fact, there does exist a counter-narrative—a kind of anti-Pocahontas—whose presence offers some small hope to the Native reader: the sign of Orpah, sister-in-

---

30. Darr, *Far More Precious*, p. 72.

31. In *The Feminine Unconventional: Four Subversive figures in Israel's Tradition* (Minneapolis: Fortress Press, 1990), Andre LaCocque observes that most biblical exegetes 'stubbornly propose' the Syriac translation of 'Ruth' as an abbreviation of *Re'uth*, or female companion. Like other scholars who have carefully studied the book of Ruth, LaCocque persuasively argues that, philologically, the name 'Ruth' has nothing to do with *r'h* (to be a companion), but rather is a cognate of *rwh* (to water to saturation). See his discussion, pp. 115-16.

law of Ruth and the woman who returned to her mother's house.

'They broke once more into loud weeping. But while Orpah kissed her mother-in-law goodbye, Ruth clung to her' (Ruth 1.14, translation by Sasson). The figure of Orpah is only mentioned twice in the book of Ruth—1.4, which names her as one of the 'Moabite wives', and 1.14, which describes her decision to part ways with Naomi and Ruth. Unfortunately, however, most contemporary scholars mimic the biblical text by leaving her to return home unattended, both literally and critically. Traditionally, Orpah generated much more scrutiny, although much of it was negative. According to midrashic literature, for example, her name allegorically connotes the opposite of Ruth's, since it originates in the root '*orep*, that is, the nape of the neck, and describes how she turns the back of her neck to Naomi when she decides to return to Moab. 'That the sages name Orpah for this moment in her history indicates that they also consider it the most important part of her story'[32]—and it explicitly charge her with the narrative role of abandoner.[33] Some writers even suggest that she later becomes the mother of Goliath, the famous enemy of Israel, and that Goliath himself was 'the son of a hundred fathers'.[34] But what else could one expect from a 'daughter of Lot?'

William Phipps expresses a more current and enlightened view of Ruth's sister-in-law:

> Orpah displays wrenching ambivalence, deciding first one way and then another. She finally takes Naomi's common-sense advice and, after an affectionate goodbye, returns 'to her people and to her gods'. Her life is difficult enough without taking responsibility for an older widow in a land presumed to be governed by a deity different from the ones she worships (the Moabite Stone refers to Chemosh and to goddess Ashtar, or Ishtar)... She does the prudent thing and heads for her family home to await an arranged remarriage.[35]

---

32. Leila Leah Bronner, 'A Thematic Approach to Ruth in Rabbinic Literature', in A. Brenner (ed.), *A Feminist Companion to Ruth* (Feminist Companion to the Bible, 3; Sheffield: Sheffield Academic Press, 1993), pp. 146-69 (155).

33. M. Bal, *Lethal Love: Feminist Literary Readings of Biblical Love Stories* (Bloomington: Indiana University Press, 1987), p. 74.

34. Bronner, 'Thematic Approach', p. 155.

35. Phipps, *Assertive Biblical Women*, p. 53.

While I do not disagree with Phipps's summary, I also believe that he fails to recognize what is perhaps the most important element of Orpah's decision. She does not just take the path of least resistance—the path of prudence, freedom from responsibility and passivity. Rather, Orpah returns to *bêt 'immāh*, 'her mother's house'.[36] Carol Meyers observes that the use of *bêt 'immāh* is quite rare in the Hebrew Bible and indicates a family setting identified with the mother rather than the father.[37] In fact, she notes, each biblical passage using this phrase shares a similarity with all the others: a woman's story is being told; women act as agents in their own destiny; the agency of women affects other characters in the narrative; the setting is domestic; and finally, a marriage is involved.[38] Meyers further concludes that all biblical references to 'the mother's house' offer female perspectives on issues that elsewhere in the Bible are viewed through a predominately androcentric lens. I would argue that the female perspective offered by 'the mother's house' in Ruth is a profoundly important one for Native women, since it signifies that Orpah—the one whose sign is the back of her neck—exists as the story's central character.

To Cherokee women, for example, Orpah connotes hope rather than perversity, because she is the one who does not reject her traditions or her sacred ancestors. Like Cherokee women have done for hundreds if not thousands of years, Orpah chooses the house of her clan and spiritual mother over the desire for another culture. In fact, Cherokee women not only chose the mother's house, they also owned it (along with the property upon which it stood as well as the gardens surrounding it). Read through these eyes, the book of Ruth tells a very different story indeed.

Ojibway poet Kimberly Blaeser illuminates this transformative process of reading through a concept she describes as 'response-ability'. In her essay, 'Pagans Rewriting the Bible', Blaeser defines

36. 'But Naomi said to her two daughters-in-law, "Go back each of you to your mother's house"' (Ruth 1.8).

37. Carol Meyers, 'Returning Home: Ruth 1.8 and the Gendering of the Book of Ruth', in Brenner (ed.), *A Feminist Companion to Ruth* (Feminist Companion to the Bible, 3; Sheffield: Sheffield Academic Press, 1993), pp. 85-114 (91).

38. Meyers, 'Returning Home', pp. 109-110.

response-ability as the need of American Indian people to 'reconsider, reevaluate, reimagine what [religious] terms might mean or have meant to Indian people as well as what they might come to mean to all people'.[39] This is precisely what Rigoberta Menchú accomplishes in her choosing of Judith over Moses and in her insistence that the meaning of any biblical text reflect her people's reality. It is also what I have tried to effect in my own rereading of Ruth through a Native perspective and, more particularly, through the perspective of Cherokee women. I have reconsidered the dominant exegesis of Ruth as either a paradigm of conversion or a woman-identified woman. I have reimagined this literary jewel of the Hebrew Bible as the narrative equivalent of a last arrow pageant.

During the implementation of the Dawes Act,[40] the 'last-arrow pageant' was a public ritual that marked the translation of American Indian identity into its more 'civilized' white counterpart. Etymologically, the word 'translation' means 'carried from one place to another', or transported across the borders between one language and another, one country and another, one culture and another.[41] In the context of last-arrow pageants, participants performed and acknowledged their own translation into the idiom of Euramerican culture:

> This conversion of Indians into individual landowners was ceremonialized at 'last-arrow' pageants. On these occasions, the Indians were ordered by the governments to attend a large assembly on the reservation. Dressed in traditional costume and carrying a bow and arrow, each Indian was individually summoned from a tepee and told to shoot an arrow. He then retreated to the tepee and re-emerged wearing 'civilized' clothing, symbolizing a crossing from

39. Kimberly M. Blaeser, 'Pagans Rewriting the Bible: Heterodoxy and the Representation of Spirituality in Native American Literature', *Review of International English Literature* 25.1 (1994), pp. 12-31 (13).

40. Passed in 1887 and named for its sponsor, Massachusetts senator Henry L. Dawes, the Dawes Act attempted to detribalize American Indians by privatizing communally held Indian lands and partitioning reservations into 160- and 80-acre lots subject to sale or lease by the government. Between 1887 and its end in 1934, the Dawes Act reduced the total land base of American Indian peoples by two-thirds.

41. J. Hillis Miller, *Topographies: Crossing Aesthetics* (Stanford, CA: Stanford University Press, 1995), p. 316.

the primitive to the modern world. Standing before a plow, the Indian was told: 'Take the handle of this plow, this act means that you have chosen to live the life of the white man—and the white man lives by work.' At the close of the ceremony, each allottee was given an American flag and a purse with the instructions: 'This purse will always say to you that the money you gain from your labor must be wisely kept.'[42]

For 'Ruth the Moabite', the translation from savagery to civilization (or from Asherah to Yahweh) similarly involves the relinquishing of her ethnic and cultural identity. For Orpah, it necessitates a courageous act of self and communal affirmation: the choosing of the indigenous mother's house over that of the alien Israelite Father.

In this interpretation, my responseability as a person of Cherokee descent and as an informed biblical reader transforms Ruth's positive value into a negative and Orpah's negative value into a positive. Such is the epistemological vertigo inspired by reading in the contact zone. Indeed, paraphrasing Blaeser, recognizes that life—or meaning in the book of Ruth—cannot be produced for easy consumption. Chinese feminist theologian Kwok Pui Lan echoes a similar sentiment in her statement that 'these attempts at indigenization [of the Bible] show clearly that biblical truth cannot be pre-packaged, that it must be found in the actual interaction between text and context in the concrete historical situation'.[43] I can only hope that my indigenization of Ruth has located new meaning in the interaction between biblical text and American Indian context—a meaning that resists imperial exegesis and contributes to the empowerment of aboriginal peoples everywhere.

42. Ronald Takaki, *A Different Mirror: A History of Multicultural America* (Boston: Little, Brown & Co., 1993), pp. 235-36.

43. Kwok Pui Lan, *Discovering the Bible in the Non-Biblical World: The Bible and Liberation* (Maryknoll, NY: Orbis Books, 1995), p. 11.

Local is Lekker, but Ubuntu is Best: Indigenous Reading Resources from a South African Perspective

GERALD O. WEST

Introduction

As the first part of my title suggests, vernacular hermeneutics is vernacular! To speak of vernacular hermeneutics is to speak of the reading strategies and resources of ordinary people. However, as soon as I 'speak of' their reading strategies and resources, vernacular hermeneutics ceases to be vernacular.

So, at the heart of vernacular hermeneutics is the relationship between the socially engaged biblical scholar and the ordinary indigenous reader. By 'ordinary reader' I mean generally, any non-specialist reader. But more specifically, I use the term to designate poor and marginalized indigenous reader/hearers of the Bible. My presence in 'speaking of' vernacular hermeneutics cannot, and must not, be elided; indeed, it must be foregrounded. This is particularly true because I am a white, middle-class, male South African, and we have too often spoken on behalf of others; but it is also true, I would argue, for those biblical scholars who are closer to ordinary indigenous readers of the Bible than I am. Our presence takes up the space and the place of the ordinary indigenous reader; we re-present her and him.

Ordinary Readers

I want to limit talk of vernacular hermeneutics to the reading strategies and resources of ordinary readers of the Bible (West 1999: 10). Biblical scholars are, by definition, not ordinary readers. We are (academically) trained readers. This is the case for those biblical scholars from the South/Third World/Two-Thirds World and those from the margins of the North/First World. Our biblical studies training marks us and makes us; we/they no longer speak a vernacular only, we/they also speak an international language.[1] While we may return to the local reading resources of our own communities, scholars do so from a quite different position. Our training gives us access to choices and resources ordinary indigenous readers do not have. This does not make us better readers of the Bible, as many of us would acknowledge, but it does make us different.

Drawing on four case studies of ordinary indigenous readers reading the Bible (West 1995a: 174-200), I have demonstrated that while there may appear to be some affinities between the reading strategies and resources of ordinary readers and the modes of reading of socially engaged biblical scholars,[2] the situation is more complex. There are certainly interesting similarities, but we must recognize that something fundamentally different is going on in the modes of reading of ordinary indigenous readers.

Ordinary readers read the Bible precritically. My use of 'precritical' is not pejorative; ordinary indigenous readers have little choice in how they read the Bible. They read it precritically because they have not been trained in the critical modes of reading that characterize biblical scholarship. There is no mystery here. Biblical scholars are trained to ask structured and systematic sets of questions (whether they be historical-critical, socio-historical, literary, structuralist, deconstructionist, canonical, etc.); and ordinary indigenous readers have not been so trained. In fact, many ordinary indigenous readers are not actually readers at all; they are illiterate hearers, interpreters and retellers of the Bible. So although there may be important similarities between the

---

1.   My use of 'we/they' reflects my own positionality. To what extent am I, a seventh-generation South African, indigenous? There is no easy answer to this question, but as this and other related questions are beginning to be debated in South Africa, some sense of the issues involved are emerging. From this point in the essay I will usually use 'we', positioning myself with other indigenous biblical scholars, a move which I will discuss below.

2.   My focus has always been on the work of socially engaged biblical scholars (engaged, for example, in liberation hermeneutics) rather than those biblical scholars who choose to hide their social commitments and interests.

modes of reading of ordinary indigenous readers and the modes of reading of trained readers, there is nevertheless this crucial difference, namely, that ordinary readers read the Bible precritically, while biblical scholars read the Bible critically (or postcritically).

This difference is crucial; but again I must stress that my use of the terms 'critical'/'precritical' carries no sense of 'better'/ 'worse'. I am using these terms in a carefully specified technical sense. My purpose is to delineate the domain of vernacular hermeneutics, and my point here is that it is to be found in the precritical reading strategies and resources of ordinary indigenous readers.

In so doing I am not denying that ordinary indigenous readers read (or hear) the Bible with a critical consciousness. Itumeleng Mosala indicates this when he argues that black scholars like Allan Boesak and others

> have been surpassed by the largely illiterate black working class and poor peasantry who have defied the canon of Scripture, with its ruling class ideological basis, by appropriating the Bible in their own way using the cultural tools emerging out of their struggle for survival (Mosala 1986: 184; see also Mofokeng 1988: 40-41).[3]

However, while there is definitely a 'critical consciousness' on the part of some ordinary indigenous readers, this is not quite the same as the socio-historical approach advocated by Mosala. Ordinary indigenous readers may, and often do, have a general critical consciousness towards society and texts, but they do not have the historical and sociological tools to be critical of the biblical text in the same way as Mosala. When young black workers in Young Christian Workers (YCW) appropriate the Bible as the story of liberation they are doing so on the basis of selected texts (and not various redactional layers) and of selected historical and sociological information (and not a systematic reconstruction of the social system behind the text) (West 1995a: 188-93). The political critical consciousness of some ordinary readers may predispose them to a critical approach to the Bible, but as ordinary readers this is not their mode of reading.

Similarly, J. Severino Croatto seems to argue that the poor and oppressed actually read the Bible in the way that his in-front-of-the-text mode of reading articulates (Croatto 1987: 50). But once

---

3.   Unfortunately Mosala does not provide any examples.

again it is important to recognize that while many ordinary readers do read the Bible thematically in its final form as a single
canonical text, this is not quite the same as the linguistic-symbolic
post-critical canonical approach of Croatto. When ordinary readers read the Bible thematically in its final form they begin with
creation (and not exodus) and read selectively (and not along 'a
semantic axis'). So while poor and marginalized ordinary indigenous readers may be predisposed to such a post-critical in-front-of-
the-text reading of the Bible, their own strategies and resources
are different.

Within vernacular hermeneutics it is crucial that we recognize
this difference. So I reserve the term vernacular hermeneutics for
the reading strategies and resources of ordinary readers of the
Bible.[4]

Representing the Other

My limiting of the term 'vernacular hermeneutics' in this way
does not mean that socially engaged biblical scholars do not participate in vernacular hermeneutics. They do; indeed, this is one
of the characteristics of vernacular hermeneutics—that socially
engaged biblical scholars are called to participate in reading the
Bible with ordinary indigenous readers. In my own South African
context our struggles against apartheid and for survival, liberation
and life have brought together ordinary indigenous Bible readers
from poor and marginalized communities and socially engaged
biblical scholars from the local university. Our initial response as
biblical scholars to the call of ordinary indigenous readers was an
overwhelming sense of the inadequacy and paucity of our
resources in this context. And yet the call of the community also
helped us to recognize that we did have resources which might be
useful, provided we were willing to read the Bible and do theology
with them. The result of our collaboration is an emerging interface in which socially engaged biblical scholars and poor and
marginalized readers of the Bible do what we call *contextual Bible
study*—a form of Bible reading that begins with an emancipatory
interest that is grounded in the real conditions of poor and

4.   See West (1999: 79-107) for a more detailed discussion of some of the
reading strategies of ordinary indigenous readers.

marginalized local communities (see West 1993a).

Our work together is guided by the basic assumption that resources for a contextual reading of the Bible are to be found *both* in biblical studies *and* in the resources of ordinary indigenous poor and marginalized communities. The experience of similar initiatives in other contexts, for example in Brazil, have demonstrated two potential problems which constantly recur in such an interface: biblical scholars either romanticize and idealize the contribution of the poor and marginalized or they minimize and rationalize the contributions of these communities and sectors (see Segundo 1985). Both these approaches are problematic: 'listening to' presupposes the speaking voice of a wholly self-knowing subject free from ideology, while 'speaking for' denies the subject status of the poor and oppressed altogether (Arnott 1991: 125).

We must problematize the notion of the pure presence or essence of, for example, 'the Third World woman' (Spivak 1988: 286). Not only is this colonized Third World woman 'irretrievably heterogeneous' (Spivak 1988: 284), but she is also linguistically and ideologically constituted. Instead of 'invocations of the *authenticity* of the Other'—in this case the Third World woman—'the mechanics of the constitution of the Other' would be more analytical and useful (Spivak 1988: 294). So we must move beyond 'listening to' and take account of the forces and factors that constitute the fractured subjectivity of, for example, the Third World woman (Spivak 1988: 278).

Even more problematic is 'speaking for'. The seduction for intellectuals, including socially engaged biblical scholars, is that their positionality is elided. The dangerousness of the intellectual lies in his or her 'masquerading as the absent nonrepresenter who lets the oppressed speak for themselves' (Spivak 1988: 292). In 'speaking for', or speaking on behalf of, the role of the intellectual in selectively constructing the subjectivity of the Other in the process of re-presenting them is hidden. In the relay race of representing the Other the temptation is for the intellectual to become transparent (Spivak 1988: 279). Socially engaged biblical scholars must move beyond 'speaking for' and mark their positionality as participating subjects.

We can only move beyond 'speaking for' and 'listening to' the poor and marginalized if we are willing to enter into a 'speaking with'.[5] I use the phrase 'speaking with', following Jill Arnott and Gayatri Spivak, to point to 'the need to occupy the dialectical space between two subject-positions, without ever allowing either to become transparent' (Arnott 1991: 125). This requires that we socially engaged biblical scholars remain constantly alert to, and interrogative of, our own positionality and that of our discourse partners, so as to ensure that the mediating process of representation remains visible. In other words, with Arnott and Spivak, I am arguing that 'speaking with' takes seriously the subjectivity of both the biblical scholar and the ordinary indigenous reader of the Bible, and all that this entails for their respective categories and contributions.

It must be continually stressed, as well, that the power relations in the interface between ordinary indigenous readers and socially engaged biblical scholars cannot be obliterated and must not be ignored. They must be foregrounded. Postmodern feminists like Arnott and Spivak emphasize the creative and constructive potential of 'a genuinely dialectical interaction between two vigilantly foregrounded subject-positions' (Arnott 1991: 127). Only then can we move beyond 'speaking for' and 'listening to' toward a place where difference enables.

So, socially engaged biblical scholars do have a role in vernacular hermeneutics. My earlier point, however, holds; as soon as we move out of collaborative work with ordinary indigenous readers of the Bible we are representing them. The call of ordinary indigenous readers, particularly the vast majority who are in poor and marginalized communities, is a call to participate *with* them *against* the forces of death and destruction and *for* the forces of survival, liberation and life. When we work and struggle together we are engaged in vernacular hermeneutics because they have invited us to do so. When we socially engaged biblical scholars write about or talk about vernacular hermeneutics in essays like this, we are re-presenting, and our representation, I would argue, is no longer vernacular.

I would also argue that it is important for us socially engaged biblical scholars to risk representation, with the agreement of

5.   Spivak uses the phrase 'speaking to', but I prefer the preposition 'with'.

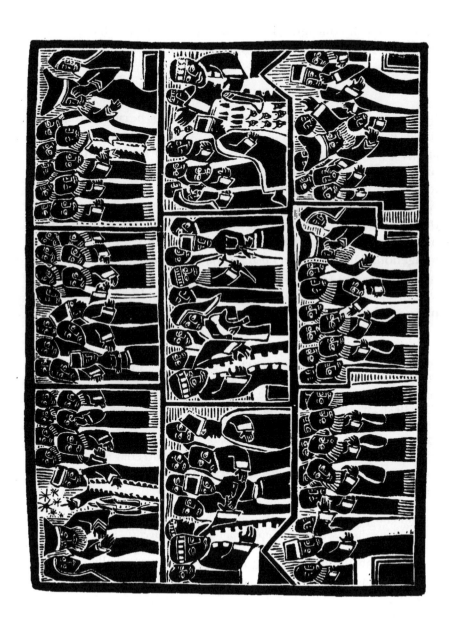

those ordinary indigenous readers we read with.[6] We must risk representation for at least two reasons. Our representations may, in some way, resonate with and be useful to ordinary indigenous readers in other contexts. Secondly, our representations are a challenge, both in terms of the reading product and the reading process, to our colleagues in the academic guild who have not yet chosen to collaborate with ordinary indigenous readers.[7]

Local Resources for Reading

I share the following example of vernacular hermeneutics for these reasons. This woodcut (see illustration) by Azaria Mbatha is an example of vernacular hermeneutics as it stands.[8] Mbatha is himself an ordinary African reader, and this is his reading of the Joseph story (Gen. 37–50). It has also become a resource for local communities of ordinary indigenous readers in our area to read the Joseph story.[9] The readings of the Joseph story represented here have all emerged from actual Bible studies with ordinary indigenous African readers using Mbatha's woodcut as a resource.

Mbatha's, and our,[10] interpretation locates the story in Africa, which is where most of the Joseph story as told in Genesis takes place, and he reads the story from and for his African context.

6.   The readings that emerge in vernacular hermeneutics may be dangerous if made public. This has certainly been the case in South Africa. Vernacular hermeneutics is often a hidden discourse—a discourse of resistance—that is spoken behind the backs of the dominant (see West 1995b; Scott 1990). When this is the case it is deeply and dangerously irresponsible for socially engaged biblical scholars to make public what is deliberately hidden.

7.   I use the term 'collaborate' quite deliberately. Terms like 'dialogue' and 'conversation' are problematic (see Schüssler Fiorenza 1989 and Eagleton 1984).

8.   The woodcut is used with the permission of the artist, and the readings with the permission of participants in the contextual Bible process.

9.   I have discussed this example from other perspectives in earlier publications (see West 1993b and 1994).

10. Given the way in which Mbatha's woodcut functioned in our contextual Bible study groups, 'Mbatha's reading' is used as a shorthand for 'our' communal reading of the Joseph story. Where appropriate I have included comments from Mbatha's own reflections on this and other works of his (Mbatha 1986).

The characters, themes and concerns are African, with the symbols and ideas coming specifically from the Zulu tradition and culture (Mbatha 1986: 6). Mbatha's reading recovers some of the Africanness of the Bible and reminds us that the Bible belongs to Africa as well as the Western world. Mbatha's reading also remembers the past, a past which 'we need to be reminded by and about', and which 'we as Africans were compelled to forget' (Mbatha 1986: 7).[11]

Mbatha's interpretation portrays the perspective of Africa in its concern for the community and in its concentration on human oppression. Every panel of the woodcut is filled with characters. This is not a story of an individual but the story of a clan and of a community. It is a story of *ubuntu*: a person is a person because of other people. But it is also a story of powerlessness and isolation (see Mbatha 1986: 7, 9).

The threat to *ubuntu* is recognized in panels 2, 4, 7 and 8 where Mbatha's interpretation 'from below' focuses on the human being as object. The panels are set out as text—from left-to-right and from top-to-bottom. In each of these panels a human is being exchanged for money; the human being is an object to be bought and sold. Panels 2 and 4 depict the two times Joseph is sold: to Ishmaelite/Midianite traders by his brothers and by the Ishmaelites/Midianites to an Egyptian officer of Pharaoh. As often happens, those who have themselves been treated as objects to be bought and sold do the same to others. So in panel 7 Joseph, who is now an important and powerful official in Egypt and who has not yet been recognized by his brothers, forces the brothers to leave Simeon behind as a hostage so that they will return to Joseph with Benjamin.[12] And as panel 8 indicates, Jacob is forced to send Benjamin as a ransom for Simeon and in exchange for food. Mbatha recognizes, and reminds us of, the

---

11. 'It was European civilization which brought the end of African civilization and replaced it with its own. I cannot find the words to describe what a terrible crime this is' (Mbatha 1986: 8).

12. Some of these Bible studies took place at the time when Nelson Mandela and others from the liberation movements were being released from prison, and there was much discussion about whether these leaders, once they held political office, would use their power to empower others or to dominate.

suffering of those who are manipulated and exploited by the powerful.

Panels 3 and 5 demonstrate the deception of the powerful and the silent presence of those who suffer. In panel 3 the brothers deceive their father and the mother of Joseph even though they know that their lie will bring great grief to them. In panel 5 Potiphar's wife deceives her husband by falsely accusing Joseph, her slave, of sexually assaulting her. Mbatha's reading remembers those who suffer the abuse of the powerful.

Mbatha's reading also probes the presence of the powerful, those 'who live in this world at the expense of the weak' (Mbatha 1986: 5). The pain of their presence in the Joseph story is amplified by his recognition that the oppression of the weak is perpetrated and perpetuated not only by those outside the community (panels 4 and 5), but also by members of the community (panels 1, 2, 3, 7 and 8). This is genuinely terrible: the recognition that the ability and will to dominate and destroy lie among us in the family and community (see Mbatha 1986: 10). *Ubuntu* is broken, families are separated and communities moved, not only by forces without but also by forces within.

By foregrounding the youngest sons, Joseph and Benjamin, in his interpretation, Mbatha recovers the story's emphasis on community continuity. 'When a child is born the chain of ancestors grows by another link' (Mbatha 1986: 21), hence the isolation, alienation, fear and hopelessness of Jacob and Leah (or Rachel, or Bilhah, or Zilpah)[13] in panels 1, 3 and 8. Not only is the continuity of community threatened, but a connecting link with the *amadlozi* (ancestors) is also lost (Mbatha 1986: 41), because the *amadlozi* often speak through young children in dreams and visions (panel 1).[14] Furthermore, a child who dies lacks the wisdom and experience of the community to become a significant ancestor who will guarantee continuity between the past and the future (see Mbatha 1986: 25).

As indicated, Mbatha explores the communal function of

13. I discuss the women in the Joseph story in more detail below.

14. I wish to acknowledge the assistance of two colleagues, Dumisani Phungula and Bafana Khumalo, in helping me to explore this point. This is also an appropriate place to acknowledge all the ordinary indigenous African readers whose readings I am representing.

dreams and interpretation (panels 1 and 6). In panel 1 Joseph is the dreamer, a link between the *amadlozi* and the future of the community, while in panel 6 the wisdom and experience which comes from suffering has enabled him to become an interpreter of dreams. In each case Mbatha offers us fresh insights into the function of dreams and their interpretation in the plot of the story.

Mbatha's panels also display his careful reading of the Joseph story. For example, his use of clothing as a symbol of power and suffering is derived from the text itself. Mbatha is using and interpreting a dominant symbol of the biblical text. Joseph's beautiful cloak separates him from his brothers and is a symbol of his father's favouritism in panel 1. But his cloak is also a symbol of conflict in the family, because it is stripped from him when he is assaulted and sold by his brothers (panel 2). The cloak, which the brothers have smeared with blood, is then used to deceive their father and mother (panel 3). As in panel 2, so in panel 4 Joseph's vulnerability and powerlessness is portrayed again by the absence of clothing. In both panels he is unclothed and naked, an object with no human dignity. Between the events of panels 4 and 5 Joseph has obviously been clothed by Potiphar, signifying his new position and power, because in panel 5 Potiphar's wife holds Joseph's garment in her hand as an accusation against him.[15] Once again clothing is used to deceive. But in panels 6, 7 and 9 Joseph is clothed once again, this time with the clothes of Egyptian favour and power.

This African reading remembers the powerful and mighty, those 'at the top', who have everything they need and who lack neither food nor comforts (Mbatha 1986: 33). This African reading also remembers 'most people', those who are weak, who are at the bottom, 'unable to clothe or feed themselves, unable to speak

---

15. There was usually considerable debate around this scene. Most readers accepted the narrator's point of view, arguing that white madams often sought sexual favours from their male servants, using their position and power to suppress any form of resistance. However, some, usually women readers, were not happy with this reading, arguing instead that this scene portrayed a typical male perspective. They were not convinced that this was the whole story.

about their own problems or to maintain the bonds to their community' (Mbatha 1986: 33).

In our readings we have also begun to develop Mbatha's theme of human beings as exchangeable and expendable objects through to the end of the story,[16] including the episode in which Joseph expropriates the land and enslaves the people (Gen. 47.13-25). We have also drawn on other African resources to recover aspects of the story which are only partially present in Mbatha's interpretation. For example, with African women we have attempted to uncover and recover the partially told story of the women characters. Although the story appears to be about a father and his sons, the movement of the plot is really determined by the respective relationships between the wives (Leah, Rachel, Bilhah and Zilpah) and their husband (Jacob) and between these mothers and their sons. And African readers do have resources in their traditions and cultures which can uncover and recover this matrilineal presence and power. For example, in probing the presence and power of women in the story we have drawn on the distinctions in Nguni culture between *indlovukazi* ('first wife': Leah), *inthandokazi* ('favourite wife': Rachel) and *isancinza* ('helper to the wife': Bilhah and Zilpah) as a resource for exploring the relationships between the women and their husband and their respective sons.

The Challenge to the Academy

These readings have emerged in an interface between ordinary indigenous African readers and socially engaged biblical scholars. In our South African context these readings matter; they shape our society. This is another characteristic of vernacular hermeneutics: our readings of the Bible are not just interesting, they are interested (see West 1992). Our readings of the Bible are resources for our struggles for survival, liberation and life, and can be heard in almost every story, for example, that is being told before the Truth and Reconciliation Commission at this very

16. Just where the story ends is an important decision for any interpretation. Mbatha's ending of hope and community healing is difficult to resist, but the textual story goes on and offers a range of other, less redemptive, endings.

time. Vernacular hermeneutics is a part of our daily reality; it happens on the streets, not in the corridors of the academy.

But, as I have indicated, there is a place here for socially engaged biblical scholars who have chosen to be partially constituted by collaborating with ordinary indigenous poor and marginalized readers of the Bible. It is not a prominent place; we and our resources are simply additional resources to be shared with the local resources already present. Some of our scholarly resources may be useful, but whether they are or not is not our decision, it is the decision of those who have called us to work with them.

In the many local communities in which we have read the Joseph story using Mbatha's woodcut I have found numerous resonances with biblical scholarship in our readings, and these have been opportunities to support and strengthen vernacular readings by offering resources from biblical scholarship. Mbatha's sustained use of clothing as a symbol of power and suffering, for example, follows the contours of the text closely, and has been noted by many scholars. Our training also enables us to assist ordinary indigenous readers to read those parts of the text that they find difficult to navigate. So, for example, when we realized that we needed to develop Mbatha's theme of human beings as exchangeable and expendable objects through to the end of the story— including the episode in which Joseph expropriates the land and enslaves the people (Gen. 47.13-25)—this proved to be rather difficult. Ordinary indigenous readers found it extremely difficult to read the final chapters of Genesis as the narrative becomes increasing disjointed and fragmented. Here they turned to us socially engaged biblical scholars to help them read to the end.

By arguing that we might have resources to offer to ordinary indigenous readers of the Bible I do not mean us to forget, as is our tendency, that they have resources of their own with which to read, as Mbatha's woodcut and the readings that it has resourced clearly demonstrate. More importantly, as we allow ourselves to be partially constituted by our work with ordinary indigenous readers we discover that their experiences and resources offer us other ways to read (West 1999). This is the real challenge of vernacular hermeneutics.

BIBLIOGRAPHY

Arnott, Jill
    1991   'French Feminism in a South African frame?: Gayatri Spivak and the Problem of "Representation" in South African Feminism', *Pretexts* 3: 118-28.

Croatto, J. Severino
    1987   *Biblical Hermeneutics: Toward a Theory of Reading as the Production of Meaning* (Maryknoll, NY: Orbis Books).

Eagleton, Terry
    1984   *The Function of Criticism: From The Spectator to Post-Structuralism* (London: Verso).

Mbatha, Azaria
    1986   *Im Herzen des Tigers: In the Heart of the Tiger* (text by Werner Eichel; Wuppertal: Peter Hammer Verlag).

Mofokeng, T.
    1988   'Black Christians, the Bible and liberation', *Journal of Black Theology* 2: 34-42.

Mosala, Itumeleng J.
    1986   'The Use of the Bible in Black Theology', in Itumeleng J. Mosala and B. Tlhagale (eds.), *The Unquestionable Right to Be Free: Essays in Black Theology* (Johannesburg: Skotaville): 175-99.

Fiorenza, Elisabeth Schüssler
    1989   'Biblical Interpretation and Critical Commitment', *ST* 43: 5-18.

Scott, James C.
    1990   *Domination and the Arts of Resistance: Hidden Transcripts* (New Haven: Yale University Press).

Segundo, Juan Luis
    1985   'The Shift within Latin American Theology', *Journal of Theology for Southern Africa* 52: 17-29.

Spivak, Gayatri C.
    1988   'Can the Subaltern Speak?', in Gary Nelson and L. Grossberg (eds.), *Marxism and the Interpretation of Culture* (London: Macmillan): 271-313.

West, Gerald O.
    1992   'Interesting and Interested Readings: Deconstruction, the Bible, and the South African Context', *Scriptura* 42: 35-49.
    1993a   *Contextual Bible Study* (Pietermaritzburg: Cluster Publications).
    1993b   'No Integrity without Contextuality: The Presence of Particularity in Biblical Hermeneutics and Pedagogy', *Scriptura* S11: 131-46.
    1994   'Difference and Dialogue: Reading the Joseph Story with Poor and Marginalized Communities in South Africa', *BibInt* 2: 152-70.
    1995a (1991) *Biblical Hermeneutics of Liberation: Modes of Reading the Bible in the South African Context* (The Bible and Liberation Series; Maryknoll, NY: Orbis Books; Cluster Publications).

1995b   'The Dumb Do Speak: Articulating Incipient Readings of the Bible in Marginalized Communities', in John W. Rogerson, Margaret Davies and M.D.R. Carroll (eds.), *The Bible and Ethics* (Sheffield: Sheffield Academic Press): 174-92.

1999   *Academy of the Poor: Towards a Dialogical Reading of the Bible* (Sheffield: Sheffield Academic Press).

Life in the Midst of Death:
Naomi, Ruth and the Plight of Indigenous Women

DALILA NAYAP-POT

Introduction

A man offered to marry Maria and give her a house in the capital if
she signed over her small piece of land to him. She did this, but he
did not keep his promise, but instead, threw her off the property.

As in other countries in the world, for three decades, brutal warfare has enveloped large portions of Central America. Tens of
thousands of innocent peasants and indigenous people have lost
their lives—particularly in Guatemala, El Salvador and Nicaragua.
Hundreds of thousands more have been pushed off their lands,
bombed out of their homes and have fled to neighbouring countries, including Belize, my birthplace, and Costa Rica, my adopted
homeland, women and children suffering the most. They have
been raped, murdered and taught to kill. They have fled from
their homes and small plots of land to an unknown destiny. It is
made worse by the impact of natural disasters—drought, earth-
quakes, typhoons, volcanic eruptions and others—upon large
segments of the population, particularly in these economically
poor nations. The exodus of masses of people completes the
destruction of families that warfare and disaster have set in
motion. In the lands where they end up 'temporarily', they are
usually herded into camps. Those that are fortunate enough to be
allowed to settle in homes, are usually greeted with suspicion and
even hostility. This was the fate of Salvadorans and Nicaraguans in
Costa Rica during long years of exile, until most of them were
allowed to return to their homelands to an uncertain future.

One part of my ministry is devoted to the women of an indigenous reservation many hours away (by bus and horseback) from

my home. This has made me very aware of the cultural and spiritual creativity of many exiles, and of indigenous women who are excluded within their own lands. The quotations in this paper are taken from a report that I wrote on the situation of the indigenous women with whom I work.

My personal situation is very different (I arrived in Costa Rica to study for the Christian ministry). Having lived and pastored there for more than eighteen years, I can understand what it feels like to be uprooted from one's land and family, to be displaced and to have to adapt to a new culture and language,[1] to be discriminated against and marginalized as an indigenous Christian woman. Yet a handful of women like me here and there, have been able to move on, despite these limitations. In the process, the Bible has been our most powerful tool and starting point.

As I began to reflect upon my situation and that of many other women in the light of the Bible, I found special significance in the experience of Naomi and Ruth. First, I have asked myself, who is the real heroine of this little book? Are heroines recognizable for being first? In the first chapter of this book, it seems to be Naomi. Ruth comes into the story almost incidentally, the last person to join the family. Yet it is Ruth who gets her name attached to the book. Indeed, in the patriarchal context of the development of the Biblical canon, is it not remarkable that we find included a book with the name of a woman—and a pagan at that, the daughter of a cursed race?[2] The biblical record states: 'No Amonite nor Moabite may enter the sanctuary, even after the tenth generation. For they did not welcome you with food and water when you came out of Egypt and hired Balaam to pronounce a curse' (Deut. 23.3-4).

Remarkable also is the way in which the book joins the life of this woman to that of a descendant of another 'pagan' woman,

---

1. English is spoken in Belize and Spanish in the rest of Central America.
2. Women in the Biblical record, from every walk of life, responded to God's call and related to their own people in diverse ways. But only four of them—Ruth, the Moabite, Esther, the queen of Persia, Judith and Susannah, the heroines of inter-testamental times—were honoured by documents named after them which eventually acquired canonical or deutero-canonical status. Is it only a coincidence that these same three women, living in a patriarchal society, placed their own sexuality at the service of God and their people?

Rahab, the prostitute of the cursed city of Jericho. Together, they become the progenitors of the Jewish Messiah, thus pointing the way to hope in the midst of desperation.

In our time, the message of the book of Ruth is downplayed by both liberal scholarship—which reduces it to an interesting piece of popular literature—and conservative evangelicalism. The latter sees in Ruth little more than an Old Testament preamble to the Jesus story.[3] This does not, however, do justice to the real message of this story. Not satisfied with these deductions, I have decided to learn from these women within their own cultural context. 'Long ago when judges ruled in Israel...' (1.1) places the narrative in a concrete historical period. Following this lead, my reflections on Ruth are rooted in the culture, spirituality and socio-political situation of the indigenous people of Central America at a particular moment in history—the end of the second millennium.[4]

Who was Ruth and what extraordinary things did she do? What can she say to us, women and men, today? More importantly, what clues does she give to women who are involved in survival situations and family crises? To persons who are forced to make choices of identity, faith and commitment, does the plight of Elimelech's family, fleeing Judea to find a better life in an alien environment speak today? Ruth challenges us in many ways, but I will mention four ways, hoping by this, to affirm our hope for those who have been uprooted and to invite those who have not experienced it, to be in solidarity with those who have. In so doing, we will join in the building of God's Kingdom. As I reflect upon Elimelech, Naomi and Ruth, I cannot help but remember my neighbours in Costa Rica, Daniel, Zinia and their children.

It happened on Thursday. As he did every working day, Daniel, the breadwinner of the family, left his house very early to do what he knew best, repair heavy machinery. As on any other day, he

---

3. Cf. Ralph Earle, *Beacon Bible Commentary* (Kansas City: Beacon Hill Press), p. 28. Commentaries such as this one, published by my own Church of the Nazarene, pay little attention to the role of Ruth, a peasant woman, and to her significant contribution to the history of salvation.

4. Whereas in indigenous society, everything is conceived and experienced as in or through the equilibrium of the whole, not individually but in community, 'modern' society separates religious from political life.

called his wife to see how she was doing and to enquire about his family. Little did he realize that this was going to be his last day on earth. A few hours later, a call from the hospital made his wife realize that she would not see him alive again. As so often happens in Latin America, workers are not insured. His boss refused to accept responsibility for this accident, even denying that Daniel worked for him. A wife and five children were left husband and fatherless and without economic protection.

I wrote the following poem to Daniel and his family. It was his birthday, and a gift was to be laid on his tomb—a rose. His wife did not allow anyone to accompany her but me, her close friend—not even her relatives, friends or children. She wanted to be with him, yet needed someone who would help her bear the pain. Someone who would understand her and also connect her with her loved one through prayer.

> Daniel, this is your birthday. We come to be with you
> and to give you this Rose;
> it was always our birthday gift to each other.
> It is here today, as you were here with us,
> and tomorrow it will be with you.
>
> We have come to tell you that,
> although you are in a different state,
> you are still a part of us.
> We come to wish you peace, love and rest.
> Like a Rose, you were born, you bloomed and you died.
> Isn't this, after all, what life is all about?
> An ancient indigenous sage once said:
> 'I break this egg and a man, or a woman, is born.
> Together they will live and together they will die.
> But they will live again. They will be born, die and be re-born.
> They will unceasingly be reborn, because death is a lie'.
>
> You are still alive, Daniel,
> because while we live you live, and life goes on:
> your sons and daughters are students, they are proud of you.
> Your wife struggles and gets ahead.
> You are an example to us your friends; and
> we testify to the fact that you and your house are getting ahead.
> Onward, Daniel, rest where you are, because we are here
> carrying your banner with joy. Thanks for being alive!

A Cultural Challenge: Ruth is a Bridge Builder

Elimelech and his family broke cultural stereotypes by throwing themselves upon the mercy of their ancient enemies. Yet it was only after his death, that his sons took a step farther by marrying two Moabite women. However, Ruth goes even further when she decides to become part of an enemy people and include in her world a family which descended from a people who had cursed her own race. In her own way, she seems to challenge life, particularly of those who seem to forget their past.

Moab and Judah descended from the same family tree, though history had divided them. Moab was born out of the union of Lot and his eldest daughter (Gen. 19.37). And while the Moabites allowed the Israelites to cross through their territory, they did not permit them to follow the kings' highway (Deut. 2.29; Num. 21.21-30; Judg. 11.17). For this grave cultural breach, they became an accursed people. Today we are seeing dramatically how ancient conflicts and profound cultural and religious perceptions are dividing people and bringing death upon millions in Rwanda, Bosnia, Sri Lanka and Latin America. We are in need of bridge builders. What should be their characteristics?

The bridges that cross the mountain chasms should be firmly anchored at both ends. Otherwise, they are useless and even dangerous. Also, they are meant for two way communication, which appears at the very end of this story. Useful bridges are not ornaments; they are meant to be trodden on. They are usually taken for granted—like Ruth was in this story. Her bridge building was what challenged her culture and affirmed her spirituality, redeeming her past and her future into the present. This though is not enough, but only a beginning.

An Ideological Challenge: Ruth Breaks Stereotypes

> Paulina has a very special husband. But he complains that his strength is giving out. 'I am very thin from sickness and concern for my wife. What is going to happen to us with so many negative things that surround us?'

Hunger in the midst of abundance
Famine and migration (1.2) are familiar to millions of people around the world. Ironically, there was famine in Bethlehem, a

'house of bread', in Ephrata, 'fruitful land'. This had traditionally been a land where wheat grew abundantly. But drought, foreign invasions, civil conflict and who knows how many other disasters, both natural and man-made, had upset the natural order of things. Then and now disasters and other natural disorders were accepted without question as a punishment of God for sins.[5] In Central America many 'very good Christians' are bound by a pagan fatalism. With all the natural wealth that there is in our countries, why is it that so many people accept poverty and deprivation as the will of God? At the same time, more and more victims are beginning to question the inevitability of their suffering and to ask questions regarding the human actions which are often the cause of 'natural disasters'. Central American coastlands become flooded every rainy season because of the senseless destruction of giant trees in the nearby mountain ranges. Changes in the ecological balance bring hurricanes which destroy even more trees.

The God who is absent and yet present

The God of Israel seems to be absent in this story, a curious fact. In the book of Judges, every time the people got into trouble, they called out to Yahweh and were rescued (cf. Judg. 3.7-9). Nothing is said about this in the book of Ruth. Is Yahweh allowing the protagonists to choose their own destiny, and to face the consequences of their decisions? Did Elimelech and his family give up too soon and head for Moab before God could intervene on their behalf? Or is this a case of 'God's salvation through human intervention'. Whatever the case, they opted to leave the land of 'the chosen people', and thus—according to the superstitions of the time—were on their own in the territory of strange gods. But was God really absent? Yahweh travelled with them. Their lengthy period of self-exile became a painful time of learning, of which we can only surmise by reading between the lines. We can be sure, however, that Yahweh was present as their teacher and companion.

As I try to understand Naomi from my own perspective and cultural context, I can sympathize with her reasons for agreeing to

5.   The Biblical record tells us that the time of the Judges, when Ruth's story took place, was one of particular apostasy and sin (Judg. 2.11-17).

move with her husband and family to greener pastures. We indigenous people, when left alone, will do anything to defend the integrity and welfare of our families. However, once Naomi lost her immediate family, her will to struggle seemed to vanish. Yahweh had abandoned her. Perhaps if she returned to Bethlehem—she must have reasoned—where there was abundance she could find her God again. So, there was still hope. Yes, she would find protection under the law of Israel in the land of her ancestors.

Life in the midst of death

Is this a contradiction in terms or a dynamic tension? In the middle of the loss of dear ones, or in the death of a lifetime relationship, it is difficult to see the hand of the God of life. Naomi, a refugee and a victim, found it almost impossible to understand how her God could bring something positive out of circumstances that seemed to be the end of her world. In times like these, we who suffer loss and marginalization in our own circumstances, need to stop to question our attitudes. Is it correct to blame God when we do not comprehend the totality of human circumstances and relationships and God's purposes in them? Significantly, the very poor in Latin America seem never to lose their faith in God. With perhaps exaggerated fatalism, they trust that God who knows best will see them through, unaware of the opportunities that God may provide to them to begin changing their lives. At the other extreme, people who do not suffer marginalization and privation fail to understand their complicity in the sufferings of others. They also turn to God to help them in their projects, without assuming responsibility for their actions and the consequences.

How do we resolve the tensions and contradictions inherent in a world of injustice and death? We can blame God. It can alleviate our consciences and be less threatening than inexplicable contradictions. One way of avoiding contradiction is to place people and ideas that we fear into neat stereotypes, which end up paralysing us at every level of human relationships, and even in relationship with the Creator. However, we should neither avoid contradictions nor allow them to become the cause of violent conflict. Dynamic tension produces energy in the midst of which God can be revealed and problematic situations confronted with the possibility of transformation. God is full of paradoxes. Divinity does not fit easily into any boxes. Yahweh is a god of contradictions—in fact, dynamic tensions. We find in the book of Ruth several dynamic tensions and God at work among them.

Yahweh is a God of life

Famine in Judah, the death of the three male bread-winners of the family, who died one after the other, seemed too much for Naomi and later on for the other two women who were left widowed. These are the kind of questions that always haunt us when death stands at our doors. *Without a doubt,* pious people of the time, *as always,* could have concluded that God was punishing them for having left the 'land of promise'. And weren't the sons being punished for marrying two women of the curse. The fact that Elimelech's name is not mentioned after his death makes me wonder whether this is not a hint that Naomi had erased him from her mind, perhaps because she blamed him for having taken them far from the land of her ancestors. Am I reading too much between the lines? The author of this book allows readers to know only a few details so that they can reach their own conclusions and learn their own lessons. Nonetheless, these questions help readers develop their own theology of life. Is it life just for the present or does it continue even after our corporal bodies are extinguished? Can there be the possibility of Ruth discovering this truth even before Naomi who kept moaning over her loved one and forgot to seek renewal in death from another perspective?

A Challenge to Community: Ruth Practices Solidarity

> Either women have been raped or they give themselves in exchange for a pair of shoes, a dress, or for someone to teach them Spanish.

Naomi was accepted, in spite of her self-rejection (1.8; 3.1)

In spite of all her loss, Naomi still had a lot to be thankful for. She had a family who cared for her. Her daughters-in-law had not abandoned her; they were working with her in the fields of Moab when the news of the end of the famine in Bethlehem reached Naomi. She had their support and conversely must have felt a certain responsibility toward them. Is this what she had in mind when she advised her daughters-in-law to return to their own families and gods? Naomi's arguments were accepted by Orpah. I work mainly with women, many of whom continue to be trapped in impossible situations because they accept what seems 'logical' and 'realistic' instead of being willing to take risks. I am not so much commenting upon Orpah's actions as questioning the facile and unthinking acceptance of 'givens' instead of taking charge of our lives in the name of Yahweh. 'Taking charge', of course, works out differently in each culture.

Jewish culture had taught Naomi that she belonged to 'the chosen people of Yahweh'. Having left her people years before and become part of a new family in an alien culture, Naomi's main concern was to return to her traditional roots, even if this meant leaving her new family behind. She was so embittered at the loss of her three male loved ones that she forgot to care for the two women in her adopted family! Self-rejection causes us to reject others, even those we love and who love us. While Naomi offered the young women their freedom, perhaps with a sense of guilt at having involved them in her family tragedy (1.13), she did not offer them the possibility of sharing the risk of a new life with her in a different land, *just as she herself had done years before.* Could she have been concerned that the two Moabite women might be ostracised by zealous Jews. Perhaps she was not up to this added problem, just as many of us women sell ourselves short because we feel inferior and end up missing the opportunity to create new communities. Or maybe she felt superior to her 'pagan' daughters, as so many 'good Christians' do. Such feelings can also break community.[6] Whatever the case, Naomi was about to learn a profitable lesson from Ruth.

Out of marginalization solidarity (1.19, 20; 2.2)
In this story, God is revealed through an alien woman. The God of the poor and oppressed, the widows and orphans, takes the form of a 'pagan' woman in order to bring faith to a 'pious' Jewess. Ruth is a humble woman, herself a widow, who chooses to share the risks of an uncertain future with another woman, who wrote her off.

To begin with, Ruth could have rejected a family of strangers, of refugees from an enemy nation (in much the same way in which refugees and aliens are being turned away or evicted today by

6.   From personal experience, I sense that many First World feminists feel this way toward their 'less liberated' sisters from the Third World.

richer nations). In marrying into a Jewish family she demonstrated a willingness to leave any tribal feelings of superiority (or inferiority) aside in favour of starting a new life. From her husband, she must have learned about Yahweh, the God of Israel. So now that her mother-in-law intended to leave her behind, she refused. Her life had been altered and even though her husband had gone, she needed to continue learning about this God of Israel. Ruth did not get discouraged even when Naomi seemed not to appreciate her loyalty and sacrifice. Upon their arrival in Bethlehem, Ruth the alien was not taken into account by the women who made a big fuss over their old friend Naomi. She might be rejected by others, but Yahweh had accepted her, as the story makes plain (cf. 1.19 and 22). Even though Naomi, used her, one might think, to resolve their economic situation (3.1-5), it was Ruth herself who decided to become the breadwinner for this little family of two women (2.1, 2).

Because Ruth gave of herself she also received. Her faith carried her forward even though she was no longer under any formal obligation to her mother-in-law. Today we need to learn from Ruth's unselfish attitude if we are to share God's life with others and build a better world for ourselves and for our children. We can learn from marginalized people; we can profit from the experience and values of people of other faiths. Together we can search for those things that we have in common. When we give we receive. When we empty ourselves we are filled.

A new kind of family
The context in which this story takes place is ripe for conflict, and conflict does happen. We meet an Israelite family, united by blood but divided by the socio-economic and political situation. As family, they seek refuge in a divided family lineage. For their part, Israelites were not encouraged to marry outside of their own race and religion, and least of all with citizens of a cursed race.[7] Ruth experiences the depth of a family relationship, not just in being with her husband in life but also beyond death. When given the

7.   This was the case for many years in Latin America, where 'mixed marriages' between Protestants and Catholics were prohibited by both sides. Such alliances were called 'worldly' in the context where I grew up, ignoring the fact that a growing number of formal marriages were actually defunct.

opportunity to begin a new family, she does it differently. In the process, she finds a new code of family wholeness. It is a new model of family that goes beyond traditional relationships, that follows an unconventional God who is ready to break stereotypes.[8]

The Challenge of Spirituality: When the Profane Becomes Sacred

> A very high index of pregnant single women have been abandoned by their men and rejected by their communities. Trying to find a solution, they place themselves under the protection of another man; but when they become pregnant again they are thrown out.

Indigenous women have an amazing creativity which comes out of generations of coping with adversity. In this they remind me of Ruth. She was not one to moan over her losses. She found comfort in serving Naomi who had lost far more. Even in a strange land, she did not sit back and wait for her new God to act, as Naomi seemed to be doing with Yahweh. She took the initiative in finding work to support them both by becoming a humble peasant gleaner.[9] In the process, she discovered a very surprising God: one who acts within human customs and traditions but also breaks cultural taboos. Although it was Naomi who, after Ruth met Boaz, immediately saw the possibilities of availing themselves of the levirate custom,[10] she counselled Ruth to break a sexual custom in

---

8.   In Latin America, an increasing number of mistreated and abandoned women have, understandably, become cynical about marriage. Various kinds of single parent, unmarried parents or polygamous relationships are more and more openly practised, often with the kind of love that may be actually absent in formal marital relationships. What these situations require is not a moralistic attitude, but a pastoral spirit of love and compassion that communicates hope.

9.   Gleaning along the edges and in the corners of fields was established by ancient Israelite law (Lev. 19.9, 10) and practised as well in other agrarian societies. It was a way of socializing wealth, of sharing the earth's bounty with the poor.

10.   The levirate tradition among people of the Middle East required that the closest male relative to a childless widow marry her and that their first born carry on the name of the dead brother. If the brother refused to fulfil this obligation, the woman was allowed by custom to place a mark of scorn upon him. This is the context of Tamar's extraordinary action toward her father-in-law (Gen. 38.13-25). In order to gain Ruth, Boaz also appeals to the

order to attract Boaz's attention. Breaking taboos may also be an act of holiness![11]

What follows is a rather sexy romance, Hebrew style. Following Naomi's knowledgeable advice, Ruth bathes and perfumes herself at the end of a day of gleaning, then draws close to the kinsman Boaz (who may now be a little drunk, 3.3), 'uncovered his feet and lay down' (3.6, 7). The action, even if taken literally, may be a Hebrew euphemism for a little higher up in a man's body.[12] The point is that Ruth makes herself sexually vulnerable, and available to her hoped-for benefactor, out of personal need and solidarity with Naomi.[13] This is very much an indigenous trait, where women will give their bodies even to enemies to protect their loved ones. Unlike in the Christian tradition, 'sex' was not a dirty word in Judaism, nor is it in my own indigenous tradition. It is a divine gift to be celebrated, enjoyed, talked about, shared, and even risked on behalf of others.

levirate law, along with a related tradition pertaining to the redemption of property (cf. Deut. 25.5-10, Lev. 25.25 and Ruth 4).

11. The world of the sacred, according to William E. Paden, is not limited to the supernatural. 'For its members, a religious world is simultaneously a) a set of objects imbued with transhuman power or significance *and* b) a matrix of obligations which upholds the world of those objects.' By merely focusing on the first aspect, revelation, students of religion have ignored the second aspect: the sacrality of all systems, and the need we all feel to uphold their integrity against violation. In religion, both have to do with 'holiness'. But sacred order can be oppressive, dealing in punishment and death for those who violate it. 'Sacredness then becomes identified with the process of de-profanising the religious life from its contamination with false contexts and values—and "purity" becomes a matter of backing out of the pollution of profane order'. William E. Paden, 'Sacrality and Integrity: "Sacred Order" as a Model for Describing Religious Worlds', in Thomas A. Indinopulos and Edward A. Yonan (eds.), *The Sacred and its Scholars: Comparative Methodologies for the Study of Primary Religious Data* (Leiden: E.J. Brill, 1996), pp. 3-18.

12. Amy-Jill Levine, 'Ruth', in Carol A. Newsom and Sharon H. Ringe (eds.), *The Woman's Bible Commentary* (Louisville, KY: Westminster/John Knox Press, 1992), p. 82.

13. The boundaries between 'sacred' and 'profane' in the human body are eating and sexuality. Particularly in patriarchal societies, 'bodily openings are border zones', according to Veikko Anttonen in 'Rethinking the Sacred: The Notions of "Human Body" and "Territory"', in Thomas A. Indinopulos and Edward A. Yonan (eds.), *The Sacred and its Scholars: Comparative Mythologies for the Study of Primary Religious Data* (Leiden: E.J. Brill, 1996), pp. 52, 53.

> Maya feminine spirituality begins in the liberation and reproduc-
> tion of life. This is sacred to them since it stems from the Giver of
> Life, and then from us, women, as portrayers of life... Throughout
> history [indigenous women] have managed to survive by obeying
> their masters...having lots of children by many different Spanish
> men was not their choice nor their will, yet they were prepared to
> outlive them...to resist the Spanish oppression by having chil-
> dren—multiplying their race in order to avoid extinction... While
> Maya women are by nature very modest with strangers, within the
> extended family they are remarkably liberated...unwed mothers
> are not marginalized as in Western societies.[14]

The biblical narrative seemingly highlights Boaz's high-mind-
edness and generosity in fulfilling the role of 'kinsman redeemer'
(cf. Deut. 25.5-9). But there may be some irony here. Reading
between the lines, Boaz is obviously attracted to Ruth—and she to
him! He is not above resorting to some manipulation to achieve
what he wants.[15] We see Yahweh thus working through human
sexuality and using human ingenuity to bring justice and protection to two women in distress, and not incidentally, happiness to a
man and a woman.

Would the story have ended differently if Ruth and Naomi had
sat back to wait for God to act? How often do we expect God to do
our 'dirty work' for us? How many times do we pray and sit on our
hands, or fail to recognize God at work in seemingly 'profane'

14. Dalila C. Nayap Pot, *Spirituality of Maya Women and Grassroots Protes-
tantism: Sources for Dialogue and Development*, dissertation presented in partial
fulfilment of the Master of Theology Degree, New College, University of
Edinburgh, Scotland (September, 1993), pp. 18, 20, 22. See Charles Gallen-
kamp, *Maya: The Riddle and Rediscovery of a Lost Civilization* (New York: Viking,
1985), pp. 128, 129; cf. Silvanus G. Morley, *The Ancient Maya* (London:
Oxford University Press, 1946), p. 34; see also Paul Sullivan, *Unfinished
Conversations: Mayas and Foreigners Between Two Wars* (New York: Knopf, 1989),
pp. 40, 41, 112-14, 338 n. 19; and cf. Barbara Tedlock, *Time and the Highland
Maya* (Albuquerque: University of New Mexico Press, 1992), p. 74.

15. The fact that manipulation was involved here, by both Naomi and
Boaz to achieve their respective aims, with Ruth as the pawn, may account for
the perceptive—perhaps ironic—blessing by the town elders in which Ruth is
likened to Rachel, Leah and Tamar, also women who have been manipulated
by men. Rachel and Leah (Ruth 4.11) were used by their father to trick Jacob
(Gen. 29.15-28). Tamar (4.12) slept with Judah, her father-in-law, to regain
her lost patrimony which belonged to her by the levirate custom (Gen. 38.6-
30). Cf. Newsom and Ringe (eds.), *Women's Bible Commentary*, pp. 82, 83.

actions? There may be times when God expects us to break barriers and taboos even when this means acting counter to social mores.

In the end, Ruth is fully accepted by Naomi and by her people. And Yahweh's actions have become manifest through the unassuming and unorthodox ministry of Ruth. She is called 'virtuous' by her future husband, and of more worth than seven sons, by the women who had earlier ignored her (cf. 1.19; 3.11; 4.14, 15). She is also accepted as co-inheritor of Elimelech's property (4.5). The closing verses tell us that Boaz and Ruth (both of 'questionable' ancestry) generate Obed, whose descendants are David and—as we learn much later—Jesus Christ the redeemer. They are part of a genealogy of Jesus (Mt. 1) that includes many flawed males and several 'impure' and ostracized women, some of whom are linked to this story. This is a preview of the life and ministry of Jesus, who consciously identified himself with marginalized people, and in particular, with outcast women.[16]

Conclusion

The plight of Naomi and Ruth, surviving within a patriarchal society with all its impositions, is not new to indigenous women in Latin America. Like Ruth, who begins as a secondary figure, but is first in the book that bears her name, many indigenous women have managed to survive despite their problems of not being recognized and valued. In the book of Ruth, there is no mention of God yet we cannot say that God was not present. We can say the same within indigenous culture and communities. Expecting to hear our name for God will be another form of imperial imposition where we are judged by the language we use rather than by the contribution we make to our communities.

It was not only Ruth who was called to unite her lineage. As human beings, we also should feel the responsibility to claim our heritage as human beings, which is, to join in the creation and recreation of humanity.

16. Albert Nolan, *Jesus Before Christianity* (Maryknoll, NY: Orbis Books, 1992 [1976]), p. 144.

African Cultural Hermeneutics

David Tuesday Adamo

Introduction[1]

In African indigenous culture, the means for dealing successfully with traditional problems like disease, sorcerers, witches, enemies and lack of success in life, have been developed. Western missionaries taught African Christians to discard these indigenous ways of handling problems without offering any concrete substitute, except the Bible. Charms, medicine, incantations, divination, sacrifices and other cultural ways of protecting, healing and liberating ourselves from the evil powers that fill African forests were hurriedly discarded in the name of Christianity. Yet we were not taught how to use that Bible as a means of protecting, healing and solving the daily problems of life. The Euro-American way of reading the Bible has not actually helped us to understand the Bible in our own context.[2]

1.   I would like to acknowledge the fact that this paper would have been impossible without the assistance of the Centre for the Study of Christianity in the Non-Western World, New College, University of Edinburgh, who offered me a research fellowship that enabled me to put these ideas together. I would also like to express my appreciation to the churches, especially the Cherubim and Seraphim and Celestial Church of Christ, the prophets and the evangelists in Nigeria who gave me the opportunity to interview them. This paper is an attempt to make sense of what I have been able to gather from these churches, and from the booklets found on sale on the streets in Nigeria.

2.   This is not an attempt to blame the Christian missionaries for African woes. Despite all the mistakes that Christian missionaries have made, it is an indisputable fact that they have been immense blessing to Africa in the area of education. They not only translated the Bible into African languages, they also taught Africans how to read the Bible in their languages and 'with their

Faced with some peculiar problems as African Christians, we searched the Bible consistently with our own eyes in order to discover whether there could be anything in the Bible that could solve our problems. In the process of reading the Bible with our own eyes, we discovered in the scripture great affinities with our own worldview and culture. We discovered in both the Hebrew Scriptures and the New Testament resemblances to events similar to African experience, especially painful experience. Examples of these activities are miracles, encounter with satanic powers, the reality of hunger and the deliverance of the oppressed. In the miracles narrated in the Bible, many means of healing were used—medicine, the mere pronouncement of words, touching, prayers and ordinary water. We then started asking questions as to how to read the Bible with our own eyes to meet our daily needs as African Christians. The attempt to answer these questions brought about the introduction of African cultural hermeneutics or vernacular hermeneutics.

The purpose of this paper is to discuss how this African cultural hermeneutics is used to interpret the book of Psalms in the African context. This essay will illustrate in the most concrete way how African indigenous churches have applied vernacular hermeneutics to the book of Psalms. In the process of reading this paper, it is important for readers to relax their ideas and misconceptions about Africa and Africans so that new ideas about African Christianity, no matter how strange and radical they might be, may receive an objective consideration. This is important since every idea is perspectival.

Definition of African Cultural Hermeneutics

African cultural hermeneutics is an approach to biblical interpretation that makes the African social cultural contexts subjects of interpretation.[3] This means that African cultural hermeneutics, like any other Third World hermeneutics, is contextual since interpretation is always done in a particular context. Specifically it means that analysis of the text is done from the perspective of

own eyes'. This enabled African Christians to read the Bible from their own cultural perspectives. Justin Ukpong, 'Reading the Bible with African Eyes', *Journal of Theology for Southern Africa* 91 (1995), pp. 3-14.

   3.   Ukpong, 'Reading the Bible', p. 5.

African worldviews and cultures.[4] African cultural hermeneutics is rereading scripture from a premeditatedly afrocentric perspective. The purpose is not only to understand the Bible and God in our African experience and culture, but also to break the hermeneutical hegemony and ideological stranglehold that Eurocentric biblical scholars have long enjoyed.[5] This is a methodology that reappraises ancient biblical tradition and African worldview, culture and life experience, with the purpose of 'correcting the effect of the cultural ideological conditioning to which Africa and Africans have been subjected'. Several terms appear synonymous with African cultural hermeneutics: inculturation hermeneutics,[6] liberation hermeneutics,[7] contextual hermeneutics,[8] Afrocentric hermeneutics[9] and vernacular hermeneutics.[10] I will not spend much time defining African cultural hermeneutics. Rather, I will demonstrate the way this type of hermeneutics is used in Nigeria.

Conditions for Doing African Cultural Hermeneutics

In order to do African cultural hermeneutics successfully, some conditions are important and should be mentioned as guide.

1. The interpreter must be an insider. This means that the would-be interpreter must be either an African or live and experience all aspects of African life in Africa. This means that it is difficult to do African cultural hermeneutics without living in Africa and going through the joy, the problems of poverty, ethnicity, hunger, communalism and other palatable and unpalatable aspects of African culture.

4. Ukpong, 'Reading the Bible', p. 6.
5. This is what Yorke calls Afrocentic hermeneutics which is very legitimate since all interpretations and theologies are perspectival. Gosnell L. Yorke, 'Biblical Hermeneutics: An Afrocentric Perspective', *Journal of Religion and Theology* 2.2 (1995), pp. 145-58.
6. Ukpong, 'Reading the Bible', p. 6.
7. Gerald West, *Biblical Hermeneutics of Liberation: Models of Reading the Bible in South African Context* (Monograph Series, 1; Pietermaritzburg: Cluster Publications, 1991).
8. West, *Biblical Hermeneutics of Liberation*.
9. Yorke, *Biblical Hermeneutics*, pp. 142-58.
10. E.g., the present volume.

2. He or she must be immersed in the content of the Bible. It is not enough just to know the content. It is absolutely necessary to believe the stories and the events of the Bible as a living faith. In other words, the biblical events are reflections of our present individual and communal life. The interpreter must be a person of faith. There must be a firm belief in the power of God's word.

3. Understanding African indigenous culture is absolutely important in doing African cultural hermeneutics. This is because African culture is part and parcel of African cultural hermeneutics. Despite the resemblance of the biblical and African cultures, there are still some distinct aspects of African culture. These aspects influence or dominate the interpretation of the Bible.

4. Faith in God who is all powerful is an important condition for African cultural hermeneutics. This faith in God is not only a belief in his existence but also in his absolute power to do and undo. He is in control and he performs miracles at will. This God can use any means to heal, protect, and bring success in all life endeavour.

5. The ability to read or memorize the words of the Bible is important. The interpreter may not necessarily be a scholar of the Bible. Some of the evangelists in Africa are illiterate, yet they use the word of God to perform miracles and wonders. Some blind evangelists memorize the Bible effectively.

The above conditions are reflected in the example of interpretation of Psalm below.

The Importance of the Book of Psalms

I choose the book of Psalms because of its important place in the Hebrew Scriptures. This is why the psalms are frequently quoted in the New Testament. The psalms are also the writings that the Christian community found the easiest to approach personally and directly in times of joy, sorrow, pain, confusion and danger.[11] B.W. Anderson was emphatic about the unique place given to the

11. Arthur Weiser, *The Psalms* (trans. Herbert Hartwell; OTL; Philadelphia: Westmister Press, 1962), p. 19.

book of Psalms by the Christian Church.

> Today in Roman Catholic and Eastern Orthodox Churches espe-
> cially where the ancient monastic usage is still preserved, the entire
> Psalter is recited once each week. In the Anglican [churches] the
> Psalter is repeated once a month. And in other churches in the
> Protestant tradition the profound influence of the Psalter is evi-
> dent in responsive reading of selected Psalms or in the singing of
> hymns. Indeed, when one considers the enriching and invigorating
> influence which the Psalms have exerted on preaching, worship
> and devotional life, it is no exaggeration for Christopher Barth to
> say that the renewal and reunion of the church, for which we are
> hoping, cannot come about without the powerful assistance of
> Psalms.[12]

The writers of Christian hymns throughout the centuries have
drawn from the well of the Psalter. Apart from its use in public
worship, individuals also have found edification and comfort,
especially in sorrow and affliction. The Psalter speaks about God,
and to God, in a unique way. That is why it is the favourite book of
all the saints.[13] Quoting Martin Luther, Weiser writes,

> To sum up: if you want to see the holy Christian Church painted in
> glowing colours and in a form which is really alive, and if you want
> this to be done in a miniature, you must get hold of the Psalter,
> and there you will have in your possession a fine, clear, pure mirror
> which will show you what Christianity really is; yea, you will find
> yourself in it and the true *'gnothi seauton' (know* thyself) God him-
> self and all his creatures, too.[14]

The unique place of the book of Psalms in the Christian
churches has influenced biblical scholars to struggle continuously
to discover the correct approach. Western scholars are champions
of this struggle. Their approaches include determining the
authors and dates of Psalms according to the superscriptions,
determining the literary types and forms, and the basic theological thoughts, and many others.

However, to many Africans who were converted to Christianity,
the above approaches by Western scholars appear too mechanical.

---

12. B.W. Anderson, *Out of Depths: The Psalms Speak for us Today* (Philadelphia: Westminster Press, 1974), p. 5.

13. Weiser, *The Psalms*, p. 19.

14. Weiser, *The Psalms*, p. 20.

Such approaches do not meet the daily needs of Africans who are confronted with what to eat, how to diffuse the power of enemies, diseases and even death. Africans, who were given the Bible and faith in God as substitutes for their traditional ways of protection, healing and success, constantly faced the question of how to use faith and the Bible in concrete and effective ways, for that protection against enemies and evil spirits, for healing sicknesses and bringing success at work, at school and in business. The answer to this question has been found by the African indigenous churches that have used an African cultural hermeneutic to discover distinctive ways of classifying the Psalms into Protective, Curative or Therapeutic, and Success Psalms and then using them in conjunction with other natural materials.

The Protective Use of Psalms

It is important to discuss protection in African indigenous culture before going on to the use of protective Psalms. The existence of evil is painfully real in the African indigenous tradition. Witches, sorcerers, wizards, evil spirits and all ill-wishers are considered enemies. The awareness of these enemies is a major source of fear and anxiety in African indigenous society. Among the Yoruba people of Nigeria, there is a belief that every person has at least one known or unknown enemy called *ota*. The activities of *ota* can bring painful consequences. It may be abnormal behaviour, sudden loss of children and property, chronic illness or even death. To express how powerful and wicked are the activities of witches, who are also enemies of society, Primate J.O.S. Ayelabola narrated the confession of a witch:

> We drink human blood in the day or night...
> We can prevent a sore from healing;
> We can make a person to lose a large some of money;
> We can reduce a great man to nothing;
> We can send a small child to heaven suddenly;
> We can cause a woman to bear born-to-die children [*abiku*].[15]

The belief in enemies as the main sources of all evil and bad occurrences is so strong that nothing happens naturally without a

15. P.A. Dopamu, *Esu: The Invisible Foe of Man* (Ijebu-Ode: Shebiotimo Publications, 1986), p. 57.

spiritual force behind it. Thus incidents like infant mortality, childlessness in women, impotence in men, accidents of any kind, dullness in school children, and all other bad things are attributed to enemies of different kinds. Constant fear and insecurity may also be caused by a hostile environment rather than malignant forces. Events such as road and fire accidents, gun-shot and knife wounds can also be caused by a hostile environment. People, therefore, go to a medicine person to prevent or protect themselves from such attacks.

Before the advent of Christianity, Africans had a cultural way of dealing with the problem of enemies and all evil ones. There were various techniques of making use of natural materials and potent words which were put to defensive and offensive use in dealing with evil ones. One of the cultural ways of protection against enemies was the use of powerful imprecatory spoken words (the so-called incantations) called *ogede* in the Yoruba language. Traditionally when an African identifies an enemy and does not have the potent words or medicine to deal with such an enemy, a medicine man *(babalawo* or *onisegun* or *oologun* in the Yoruba language) is consulted who prepares or teaches the person some potent words or gives a charm for protection, or for attacking the enemy. A perfect example of the type of potent words used among Yoruba society to make a sorcerer lose his or her senses is stated below:

> *Igbagbe se oro ko lewe* (3 times)
> *Igbagbe se afomo ko legbo* (3 times)
> *Igbagbe se Olodumare ko ranti la ese pepeye* (3 times)
> *Nijo ti pepeye ba daran egba igbe hoho ni imu bo 'nu*
> *Ki igbagbe se lagbaja omo laghaja ko maa wagbo lo*
> *Tori t 'odo ba nsan ki iwo ehin moo*

Translation:

> Due to forgetfulness the Oro [cactus] plant has
>   no leaves (3 times)
> Due to forgetfulness the Afomo [mistletoe] plant
>   has no roots (3 times)
> Due to forgetfulness god did not remember to
>   separate the toes of the duck (3 times)
> When the duck is beaten it cries, hoho

> May forgetfulness come upon [name the enemy],
>   the son/daughter of [name the mother];
> that is, may he lose his senses.
> That he or she may enter into the bush
> Because a flowing river does not flow backwards
>   [and so on].

The above potent words can be repeated two or three times or more without any addition.

Another major way of obtaining protection against enemies is the use of charms or amulets. The medicine men and women who are healers and diviners usually prepare amulets and charms for those who need them. They are used for diverse purposes, but mainly as protective devices to prevent enemies, witches, wizards and evil spirits from entering a house and attacking a person. They are also used to nullify all the efforts of enemies or sorcerers. They contain different ingredients depending on the purpose. For example, a charm for hanging on the door frame for protection is made of seven leaves of some plants, and seven seeds of alligator pepper. Charms to be tied around one's neck, for protection against enemies, may require alligator peppers, white and red cola nuts and the blood of a cock. Charms are wrapped with animal skin and sewn round. Others are wrapped inside pieces of cloth or paper and tied with some black and white threads. Some also require the recitation of potent words and prayers to make the charm effective.[16] These words must be recited exactly according to the prescription of the medicine man otherwise it may not be efficacious. A person can obtain charms to protect against motor accidents and crashes. In traditional Africa, hunters who hunt in the bush at night will normally protect themselves with charms against wild animal attack, snake bites, and against wicked supernatural beings such as *iwin* and *aunjonu*.

Identification of Protective Psalms in African Indigenous Churches

African converts to Christianity were forbidden to practise African cultural ways of protection because they were labelled as paganistic

---

16. S. Ademiluka, 'The Use of Psalms in African Context' (MA Thesis, University of Ilorin, 1991).

and abominable to God. Unfortunately the type of Western Christianity brought by the missionaries provided no substitute protection. At one point among the Yoruba people of Nigeria, men who accepted this type of Christianity without arming themselves with African power of words, amulets and charms were ridiculed and called women. To the Yoruba non-Christians Christianity was an impotent religion. More unfortunate was the fact that the Western Christianity that was introduced to Africans did not reveal the secrets of Western power and knowledge, but instead revealed prejudice and oppression in missionary support for colonial masters. This type of Christianity did not meet the needs of the Africans—protection, healing and success. They started to suspect that there must be more to Christianity than the missionaries had revealed. African indigenous Christians searched vigorously for that hidden treasure in the missionary religion. They sought it in the Bible, in their own way, and in their own culture. Using African cultural hermeneutics to interpret the Bible, they found secret powers in the Bible, especially in the book of Psalms. They used the Bible protectively, therapeutically and successfully to fill the missing gap left by Eurocentric Christianity. As they searched the Bible to find potent words for protection against the perennial problem of witches and all evil forces, they suddenly discovered some words in the book of Psalms that resembled the ones used in African tradition against enemies. They discovered that the words of these Psalms were not only potent—they lent themselves to imprecatory use like that found in African tradition. They classified Psalms 5, 6, 28, 35, 37, 54, 55, 83, 109 as protective Psalms. Some of them have imprecatory content. Most of these Psalms belong to the classification of the individual and community lament. They reflect the individual and the community cry to God with lament, confession, trust, petition and the promise of praise.[17]

The following are Psalms that contain curses against the enemies of the Psalmist and rejoice over the enemies' downfall:

> Make them bear their guilt O God;
> Let them fall by their own counsels,
> because of their many transgressions

17. Claus Westermann, *Praise and Lament in the Psalms* (trans. K.R. Crim and Richard N. Soulen; Atlanta: John Knox Press, 1981), pp. 52, 64.

> All my enemies shall be shamed
> and sorely troubled; they shall turn
> back and be put to shame in a moment (RSV 5.10).

Sometimes the Psalmists invoke death to come upon their enemies. Psalm 55.15, 23 says:

> Let death come upon them;
> Let them go down to Sheol alive;
> Let them go away in terror into their grave...
> (they) shall not live out half their days (RSV).

They regarded this Psalm as a Psalm for protection against enemies, since it makes them 'die by their own evil deeds'.[18] This Psalm should be read every day. The holy name of God *Jah* should be pronounced after each reading of the Psalm. The belief in God's saving grace is important as one reads this Psalm. It will protect a person against the plans of enemies. They will perish by their own evil deeds. Chief J.O. Ogunfuye prescribes Psalm 109 for use against enemies. According to him, one will need to go to an open field in the middle of the night or at 1pm. Three candles should be lit, one in the North, one in the East, and one in the West, while standing in the middle. The Psalm is read with the name of *El*, the name of the enemy, and that of his or her mother in mind. Then, pray the following prayer:

> Almighty God [name your enemy],
> the son or daughter of [name his or her mother]
> is after me to destroy me.
> Oh Lord of hosts,
> I beseech in thy mercy...
> to help me. Arise for my defence...
> Let his or her wicked deeds come back to him/her
> And let him/her perish in his/her evil designs
> Put him/her to shame...[19]

In African contexts, Psalm 35 is used imprecatorily to defeat the evil plans of enemies and especially witches and evil men. It is read in conjunction with prayers between midnight and 3am in the night in the open air while the reader is naked. As in the Yoruba tradition, Psalms are also made into amulets to be worn

18. Chief J.O. Ogunfuye, *The Secrets of the Uses of Psalms* (Ibadan: Ogunfuye Publication, n.d.), p. 37

19. Ogunfuye, *The Secrets of the Uses*, p. 66.

around the neck or around the body. Chief Ogunfuye specializes in the making of Psalms into amulets for different usages. For protection against enemies and the evil one, he prescribes Psalm 7. According to him, there are two ways to prepare this Psalm for defending oneself against secret enemies or evil forces. A person should read this Psalm with the holy name *Eel Elikon* with a special prayer every day. Below is the prayer to accompany this Psalm:

> O merciful Father, Almighty and everlasting King,
> I beseech Thee in the holy name of Eel Elijon to deliver
> me from all secret enemies and evil spirits
> that plan my destruction always.
> Protect me from their onslaught and let their evil forces
> be turned back upon them
> Let their expectation come to nought and let them fail
> in their bid to injure me.
> Let their ways be dark and slippery and let thy holy angels
> disperse them so that they may not come nigh unto my
> dwelling place. Hear my prayer now for the sake of holy Eel Elijon.[20]

Some prophets of the indigenous churches prescribed Psalms for the prevention of flood catastrophes, fire disasters, protection of soldiers in the battle field, police officers and hunters. Psalm 60 is one of the Psalms prescribed for such people and should be read with the name *Jah.*[21]

Indigenous Therapeutic System

Before the advent of Christianity and Western medicine, Africans developed some effective ways of rescuing themselves from certain types of diseases. These ways included the use of herbs, mysterious or potent words, animal parts, living and non-living things, water, fasting, prayers, laying on of hands, and other rituals for restoration of harmony between people and the environment.

Massage, as a therapeutic system, is another important way of healing which is effective in the treatment of nervous and muscular systems and especially gynaecological problems.[22] Hydrothe-

20. Ogunfuye, *The Secrets of the Uses*, p. 7.
21. J.A. Bolarinwa, *Potency and Efficacy of Psalms* (Ibadan: Oluseyi Press, n.d), p. 8.
22. J. Ubrurhe, 'Life and Healing Processes in Urhobo Medicine', *Humanitas* NS 1 (1994), pp. 6-13.

rapy involves the use of hot and cold water. Compresses and steam vapour baths can be used for different diseases like headaches, fevers, rheumatism and general pains. Hot water relaxes the skin capillaries and stimulates the activity of the sweat glands.[23] Water increases the consumption of oxygen up to about 75% and it eliminates about 85% of carbon dioxide in the body.[24]

Fasting is an important aspect of indigenous therapeutic methods in Africa. To cure an ailment, patients are instructed to abstain from food for a certain period of days or weeks. This method is usually used for curing obesity, indigestion and some mental illness and chronic diseases. Mume was very sure of the good result of fasting in curing diseases. He says that fasting is,

> The most effective means of body house cleaning known. Fasting is an eliminator of accumulated toxins as well as a general restorative. Fasting is a purifying process. It brings about a rapid elimination of toxic elements and poisonous materials from the body.[25]

Another important method of healing is what we may call faith-healing. In African indigenous religion, especially in ancestor worship, a person who is tortured by the ancestors is asked to confess and make sacrifices. After all this has been done, the offender is made to believe that he has been forgiven and healed of the sickness.

There are medicines for various conditions, such as snake bites, scorpion stings, safe delivery for pregnant women and sharp memory for students. After chewing seven alligator peppers and placing one's mouth on the patient's navel one should recite the potent words below to cure scorpion stings and headaches:

> *Oorun lode l'alamu wonu,*
> *Oorun kuju alaamu jade* (7 times)

Translation:

> When the sun is hot the female lizard
> disappears; when the sun softens, the female lizard
> appears (7 times).[26]

23. Ubrurhe, 'Life and Healing Processes', p. 12.
24. Ubrurhe, 'Life and Healing Processes', p. 12.
25. J.O. Mume, *Traditional Medicine in Nigeria* (Agbarho: Jom Trado-medical Naturopathic Hospital, 1978), p. 65. Eight therapeutic methods in Urhobo medicine are mentioned by Mume.
26. Ademiluka, 'The Use of Psalms', p. 80.

As soon as a woman who has a history of miscarriages or infant mortality is aware that she is pregnant, she should start using a concoction for pregnant women called *Agbo aboyun*. Important potent words for the purpose of safe delivery are:

> *Kankan l'ewe ina njomo*
> *Kan kan ni ki lagbaja omo lagbaja*
> *bi mo re loni*
> *Konu koho ki roju ti fifi aso re toro*
> *Ki laghaja omo laghaja a ma*
> *roju ti ofi bi omo re loni.*

Translation:

> The leaf of *ina* burns in haste
> [name the labouring woman]
> the daughter of [name her mother]
> should deliver her child in haste today
> The Konu koho tree does not hesitate
> to give off its cloth bark [name the labouring woman]
> The daughter of [name the mother]
> should not hesitate to deliver her child today
> Because the snake sheds its skin easily.[27]

Identification of Therapeutic Psalms

As stated above, with the advent of Christianity to Africa, the indigenous therapeutic method was considered not only barbaric, but an abomination to Christianity. However, the discovery of the Psalter's potency for healing aroused great interest. Some Psalms are, therefore, classified as therapeutic Psalms. The readings of such Psalms are combined with African indigenous methods of healing. Absolute faith in the word of God and in God himself is maintained but with the combination of herbs, prayer, fasting and the use of the name of God in the healing process. It is believed that virtually all types of illnesses are curable with the combination of reading Psalms and the use of African materials.

According to Adeboyejo, Psalm 1, 2 and 3 are special Psalms for stomach pain. According to him for these Psalms to be effective one should read them

---

27. Ogunfuye, *The Secrets of the Uses*, pp. 72-73.

into water with Holy name *WALOLA ASABATA JAH* (84 times),
Fried oil, potash, small salt and one egg, drink it small.
He will get all right.[28]

For a swollen stomach, he recommends Psalms 20 and 40. One should get water from a flowing river into a new pot. Put together a complete palm frond and three newly grown palm leaves in the pot. While reading Psalms 20 and 40, with the holy name *Eli Safatan* (62 times), one should light nine candles. The reader should bathe with the water for nine days.[29] Or one could read these Psalms into a mixture of fried oil, coconut oil, some cow urine and cheer oil. The holy name above could be read over it and it could be used for drinking, bathing and rubbing over the body.[30] Bolarinwa believes that these Psalms are potent in curing toothache, headache and backache. For toothache, these Psalms could be read into lukewarm water and the mouth rinsed with it until the tumbler is empty.[31] The process could be repeated from time to time.

For barren women to have children, Psalm 51, Gen. 15.1-5; 21.1-8, 1 Sam. 1.9-20 should be read three times into coconut water or raw native egg with prayer and the water drunk.[32] The action above should be done very early in the morning and naked after a woman might have known her husband. The following names should be called for effectiveness: *Jehovah Shiklo-hirami* (21 times) and *Holy Mary* (12 times).

Chief Oguntuye recognizes Psalm 6 as one to relieve a sick person of pains and worries. It is also good for stomach trouble, eye trouble or any ailment. The sick person should read the Psalm in great humility and with special prayer and the mention of the holy names *Jaschaja*; *Bali*; *Hashina*. According to him all the sufferer's worries will be removed. Below is the special prayer to be offered to accompany this Psalm for effective healing:

28. T.M. Adeboyejo, *Saint Michael Prayer Book* (Lagos: Neye Ade & Sons, 1988), p. 21.

29. Adeboyejo, *Saint Michael Prayer Book*, p. 21.

30. Adeboyejo, *Saint Michael Prayer Book*, p. 21.

31. Bolarinwa, *Potency and Efficacy of Psalms*, p. 9.

32. Prophet Sam Akin Adewole, *The Revelation of God for 1992 and the Years Ahead* (Lagos: Sam Adewole, 1991), p. 22.

O Lord God and Prince of Peace, I beseech Thee in the name of
Jaschaja, Bali, Hashina to hear me and speedily heal me from this
disease that troubles me (name the disease). Wipe away my tears
and turn my sorrow into joy. Give unto me Thy wonderful grace
to overcome all manner of diseases. Restore unto me my former health
and silence all my adversaries for ever. Forgive me all my sins and
sustain me with Thy grace all the days of my life.
Pour thy blessings upon me from above and let my prayers
be acceptable in Thy sight so that I may glorify Thy holy name
for ever. Amen.[33]

If the patient does not know how to read, someone should read
for him or her but his or her name and the name of his or her
mother must be mentioned.

A major problem in Africa is barrenness and infant mortality.
This is a cause of much family break-up and polygamy. In most
indigenous societies in Africa, priests and diviners are contacted
before any marriage contract to make sure that the spouse will
not be barren or face infant mortality. Some therapeutic Psalms
been identified as effective cures for such problems.

Psalm 1, which compares the way of the wicked with the righteous, is used therapeutically to cure gynaecological problems
such as miscarriage. Immediately a woman is aware that she is
pregnant, she should read Psalm 1 daily, in the morning and in
the evening. The process should be accompanied by prayer in the
name of *Eli-Ishaddi, Jehovah shalom.*[34]

Psalm 126, which is a prayer to God to restore Israelite fortunes,
is said to be efficacious for infant mortality.[35] A woman who has
experienced infant mortality should start reading this Psalm
immediately she is aware of her pregnancy. It should be read daily
into water for bathing, washing and drinking throughout the
period of her pregnancy. The same process should also continue
immediately after delivery to wash the baby until it is fully grown.
With the reading of this Psalm as instructed, the early death of
such a child is unthinkable. Psalm 126 could also be written on
four pure parchments, together with the holy names *Sinni, Sinsuni*
and *Semanflaf.* It should be kept in the four corners of a house
whenever pregnancy occurs and still-birth is a danger (*abiku* in

33. Ogunfuye, *The Secrets of the Uses,* pp. 5-6.
34. Bolarinwa, *Potency and Efficacy of Psalms,* p. 7.
35. Bolarinwa, *Potency and Efficacy of Psalms,* p. 67.

Yoruba and *ogbanje* in Ibo of Nigeria). Psalm 16 is recommended for safe and easy delivery. It is to be read three times, over water for drinking and bathing, by a pregnant woman with holy name *Jehovah Jarrabbillah* three times.[36]

These therapeutic Psalms are many and are also prescribed according to the type of illness. Psalms for fearfulness (127), chronic diseases (21), overdue pregnancy (27, 28, 29, 16), epilepsy (100, 109, 102) are examples. It is certain that these methods of reading Psalms therapeutically are dictated by African cultural influences on indigenous Christians. The attempt to classify the entire Bible to meet the daily needs of African indigenous Christians is still ongoing, not only because modern medicine is not available or may never be available to all in Africa, but also because indigenous medicine is effective and Christian.

Indigenous System for Securing Sucess

The examination of the classification of some Psalms as success Psalms will be more intelligible with the discussion of the use of medicine and potent words to enhance success in all aspects of life in African indigenous tradition.

Success is an important aspect of Nigerian society—success in academic life (especially passing exams), business, a journey, securing love from a person and success in court cases. Lack of success is viewed with great seriousness. African indigenous medicine for activating or improving memory abounds. Such medicine, among the Yoruba people of Nigeria, is called *isoye*, 'quickening the memory or intelligence'.[37] Below is an example of such medicine prescribed to one of my former students, for success in examinations, by a traditional healer:

> A combination of honey, eeran leaves, awerepepe leaves and one alligator pepper.
> All should be burnt together and mixed with honey.
> The client licks from the concoction and spits it into his left palm.

There is a firm assurance that the client will be successful in the examination.

Another important way by which African indigenous people try

36. Adeboyejo, *Saint Michael Prayer Book*, p. 15.
37. Ademiluka, 'The Use of Psalms', p. 88.

to bring success to themselves is the use of medicine called *awure* in Yoruba. It literally means the thing that activates success or what uncovers success. This type of medicine that brings good luck may be in the form of potent words, soap or a mixture of herbs and other ingredients to make a concoction. Whenever an important venture is being embarked upon, there is, in African indigenous tradition, a strong awareness that enemies abound. This thought is indisputable in a typical African traditional society. Hence, when there is an important venture like business, building houses, marriage, hunting for a new job or attending an interview, a medicine man is often consulted to narrow down the chances of failure and increase the chances of success.

Identifications of Success Psalms
Psalms that are identified as success Psalms are those believed by the African indigenous churches to have the power to bring success if used with faith, rituals, such as prayer, fasting and the rehearsal of some specific symbols, and a combination of other animate or inanimate materials. Christians in Africa who were not comfortable in using purely indigenous ways of obtaining success—mostly because of the condemnation by the Western orthodox Christians and missionaries—had no choice but to find an alternative method of achieving success. They turned to the Christian Bible, and found in the Psalms equivalent, if not greater, powers than those they had discarded.

For success in examinations or studies, Psalms 4; 8.1-9; 9; 23; 24; 27; 46; 51; 119.9-16; 134; are identified. For students who want to improve their memory and be sure of success in all their examinations, Psalm 4 should be used with this instruction:

> cut four candles into three each,
> light them round and be in the middle of the candles,
> put some salts under each candle, read Psalm 4 eight times.
> Call Holy Name ALATULA JA AJARAHLIAH 72 times.
> Pray for success. You will surely pass.[38]

Psalm 8.1-9 is also recommended for success in examinations.[39] The name of the school where the examination is to be taken should be written on parchment paper. At the bottom of the

38. Adeboyejo, *Saint Michael Prayer Book*, p. 23.
39. Adeboyejo, *Saint Michael Prayer Book*, p. 23.

paper write the following holy names: *Jah-Jubrillah, Elli-Apejubba, Elli-Majjubbah, Elli-Jah-bubbih, Elli-Ilah* (mention the name of the person who is taking the examination and the name of the place where the examination is taking place). Mention also *Jehovah Ellisaittah* three times (Amen) Sellah. Burn the paper to ashes, divide into two, one inside water for drinking before going to the examination and the remainder should be put in olive oil or perfume called *bintu* for anointing oneself. It is sure that the person writing the examination will pass.

In order to sharpen one's memory, Psalms 9, 24, 27 and 46 are recommended by the prophet Sam Akin Adewole, with specific instructions to be followed.[40]

> The water from 7 coconuts should be used to boil 3 native eggs. The water should be kept safely in a bowl and the eggs in another white dish. Put honey (in a bottle) close to the materials. Light seven candles round the children, preferably in the Mercy Land or Church or in your prayer room. Burn heavy incense and sprinkle original perfume. Sing 3 songs for forgiveness, 3 for mercy, and the last for thanks. Call the following Holy names: Jah-Jehova (7 times), Jesus Christ
>
> Holy Mother Mary (7 times)
> Jehova Shico Hiramy (7times)
> Jehovah Ellion (7 times)
> Jehova Jireh (7 times)
> El-braka-bred-El
> Psalms 51, 27, 24, 9, 46, Isa. 60, 2 Chron. 9.13-28 should be read.

The whole ritual should start on Tuesday night and lasts until Thursday night. If there are many children in the house, use three eggs for each of them for three days after the process. With a candle in their hands, use the candle to pray for them after each vigil. This should be repeated monthly, with the prophet's loin-cloth or girdle to wipe their heads and pray for them. With this the students will be successful. In another booklet the prophet Adewole prescribed Psalms 23 and 51 (to be read in conjunction with 1 Kgs 3.1-14)[41] for students to sharpen their memory for them to be successful in examinations.

40. S.A. Adewole, *Awake Celetians, Satan is Nearer* (Lagos: Celetia Church of Christ, Opopo-Igbala, Ikola Rd, 1991), pp. 46, 47.
41. Adewole, *The Revelation of God for 1992*, p. 24.

In a similar way to the above, but this time in one's personal life, Psalm 133 is classified as the one that will help to secure the love of a woman or a man. For example if any man is looking for a girlfriend or a wife and has a history of failure in such endeavours, or if a woman is looking for a boyfriend or a husband or if a wife is losing the love of her husband, or if a husband is looking for the love of his spouse who may be on the verge of divorce, he or she should read this Psalm with the following important instruction:

> Draw some water with your mouth into a bottle. Put some water that will fill the bottle into a bowl. Wash your face and armpit seven times in the water in the bowl. Add that water in the bowl to the water in the bottle to fill it up. Then call the name of the woman or man and the name Eve or Adam 21 times. Read Psalms 133, Ruth 1.16-17 and Solomon [song] 3.1-11 and John 1.1-4 into the water at midnight and if the person is known, give the water to her/him to drink.[42]

Chief Oguntuye recommends this Psalm 133 for husband and wife, family, society or church to avoid disharmony.[43]

In similar ways, for success in court cases, Psalms 13, 35, 46, 51, 77, 83, 87, 91, 110, 121 and 148 are recommended. For success in business, Psalms 4, 108 and 114 are recommended.

A Critical Evaluation of the Use of Psalms in African Indigenous Churches

The division of Psalms into types in African indigenous churches is informed mostly by the contents of the Psalms as understood by African Christians—lay people, prophets, pastors and evangelists. Some of the Psalms that are called Protective Psalms belong to what scholars of form criticism called the individual and community lament. The contents of these Psalms are mainly the cries of God's people and the wish for their prayers to be answered by eliminating enemies.[44] The Therapeutic Psalms are those which belong to the combination of the Western classifications of the

---

42. Adeboyejo, *Saint Michael Prayer Book*, p. 27.

43. Ogunfuye, *The Secrets of the Uses*, pp. 88-89.

44. Some of the contents of these Psalms has been discused and quoted previously.

individual and communal lament, thanksgiving, wisdom hymns and praise of God. Success Psalms include all kinds of Western classifications such as praise, lament and wisdom.

A close examination of the use of Psalms in African indigenous churches shows that the use of names is predominant. Some of the names that are recited or invoked are names of God, such as *Yahweh, Elohim, Adonai*; names of angels such as Gabriel, Michael, Uriel; and there are some unknown names such as *Alatulah, Ja, Ajarahlial, Ehala, Selidira, Tabbih, Jaschaja, Bali, Hashina Walola, Asabata Ja,* and *womwomwoba.* During my visit to some of these indigenous churches, I found out that some of the names used are names of God that describe his activities such as *Jehovah Jireh,*[45] *Jehovah Nissi, Jehovah Shallom, Jehovah Shammah, Jehovah Tsidkenu,*[46] *Jehovah Rophe,*[47] *El Shaddai, Hehovah Mkeddesh, Jehovah Rohi,*[48] *Jehovah Shaphat,*[49] *Jehovah Zadak,*[50] *Jehovah Zabad, Jehovah Emmanuel.*[51] In addition, names of enemies, judges and others, are generally mentioned. Although some of these names are from the Hebrew Scriptures, they are not properly spelled or pronounced. This is probably because the users are not literate in biblical Hebrew. However, during my interview with some of the prophets and apostles of these churches, it was claimed that these names were revealed. The truth is that some of these names are unbiblical and unknown to me and many other scholars and pastors of the mainline missionary churches in Africa. Despite the

45. The name Jehovah Jireh is to be used for special prayer to seek God's favour by reading Psalm 123.

46. This name means God is righteous and should be used for deliverance when afflicted by principalities and powers. It should be combined with the reading of Psalm 88. The name should be chanted seven times.

47. This names means Yahweh Heals (Exod. 15.26) and should be used for sick persons using clear rain water in the calabash with new palm tree leaves that point to the sky and with seven candles round the calabash.

48. This name means God is my shepherd and is to be chanted seven times with the reading of Psalm 23 for protection.

49. This name should be chanted seven times with the reading of Psalm 7 for court cases.

50. Call this name seven times against those who hated and oppressed you unjustly with the reading of Psalm 12.

51. Some of these names are not invented, they are biblical names in Hebrew.

fact that some of these names are not known, the invocation of names in the use of Psalms is quite in line with African culture, as well as with the Bible.[52]

Among Africans, names are not only symbolic, they represent the totality of persons. The Yoruba people of Nigeria regard names as having special power. Names are chosen with great care because such names may represent one's prayer to God, to the divinities. It may be an expression of faith in the existence of God (*Orunbe*), God's goodness (*Chukwu dima*), God's providence (*'Yiopese*) or God's love (*Olufemi*).[53] Names may represent the parent's experience in life or during birth. Usually, names are not given without special meanings. This is also true among the Ibos of Nigeria.[54] The very important and elaborate naming ceremony, performed among the Yoruba people of Nigeria, signifies how important names are among them. It is also believed that the type of names given to a person may change his or her destiny. Since names represent the totality of what a person is, it is believed that if you know the actual names and appellation of a person, you can make him dance to your wishes. Hence, when I was growing up in my village, if a stranger called a name, no one answered because one's heart might have been taken. I believe that African indigenous churches, by placing so much emphasis on names and the inclusion of these names of God, angels, persons in their reading of Psalms, are making effective use of the African concepts of names and power. In order to demonstrate this special power, in the names for God and the Bible, these evangelists and prophets recommend the use of these names in conjunction with the reading of specific Psalms. Different names

52. In the Old Testament, the proclamation of the names of God (Yahweh) is very frequent and is associated with his presence and power. See Psalms 20.1; 28.1; 29; 46.7, 48.8; 54.1; 59.5; 69.6; 76.1; 82; 89.6-52; 103.20; 111.9; 148.1-9; Isa. 6.2-3; 1 Kgs 22.19; Exod. 7.4; 12.41; Num. 10.36; 1 Sam. 17.45; 2 Sam. 6.2. See more lists of these passages in Weiser, *The Psalms*.

53. Unfortunately, most of the early missionaries to Africa did not care to understand the importance of these African names, but made us change our names at random. If they had understood these names, I believe that they would have taught us to choose the equivalent in the Hebrew Scriptures.

54. For further details about the significance of names, consult Roland Agoro, *Sixteen Names of God* (Ibadan: Olapade Agoro Investment Co. Ltd, 1984).

of God are used in the Hebrew Scriptures and the New Testament. Christians and disciples are asked to pray in the name of Jesus and whatever is asked in Jesus' name shall be given. Although there are some strange and mysterious names, total condemnation of this practice should be avoided, especially when God's names are included. African Christians are comfortable using these names that are believed to have abundant powers.

The use of Protective Psalms with medicine is an important aspect of the prescription for protection, success and healing. This includes the use of herbs and parts of living and non-living things, in conjunction with the reading of specific Psalms, burning candles, prayers and recitation of the names of God a certain number of times. The classification of Psalms into Protective and Therapeutic Psalms is done according to the African ways of classification of medicine. The truth is that most of the herbs used contain some potent ingredients in themselves that heal diseases. The use of non-living things may not contain any special ingredient for healing, but, from my interview, I could gather that the use of those non-living items like sand, stone and others is a demonstration of faith in God's power to make those things potent. It is also a demonstration of God's power over nature. It means, therefore, that once they are blessed, God transfers power into anything that the prophets lay their hands on.

The use of herbs and other materials therapeutically does not only have an African cultural basis, it also has a biblical basis. 2 Kings 4 shows that Elisha healed the Shunammite boy simply with words in form of prayer. He healed those who ate the poisonous herbs by casting a 'meal' into the pot to be eaten (2 Kgs 4.38-49). The flowing water from the river Jordan was also prescribed for Naaman to dip himself in seven times, and he was healed (2 Kgs 5.14). The prophet Isaiah prescribed a lump of figs for Hezekiah with the combination of prayers for his boil, and he was healed (2 Kgs 20.1-11).

In the New Testament, Jesus healed the sick with a variety of methods. He healed a leper with the mere pronouncement of potent words, 'be thou clean', and by a touch (Mt. 8.3). He healed those who were possessed with evil spirits simply with the word, 'Go'. A blind man was also healed with saliva, clay, water and potent words (Jn 9.6-7). After washing in the water of Siloam,

the blind man's eyes were opened. Paul, the apostle, also demonstrated the use of potent words. He healed Publius who was sick of
fever and a bloody flux (Acts 28.8). Peter also healed Aeneas by
the use of words and the name of Jesus.[55]

At an initial glance, the above approaches to Psalms are prone
to condemnation as paganistic, magical and syncretistic, but critical examination of the practice shows that it happened because
Western culture no longer commanded awe and admiration and
Africans had to search for true, original Christianity to deal with
both old and new African problems. The discussion above is a
perfect example of contextualization at work and Africans'
attempts to make their own contributions to Christianity. In doing
this, indigenous African Christians recognize the fact that God's
revelation at all times has never failed to take the culture of the
people seriously. In the Hebrew Scriptures, the culture of ancient
Near East was taken seriously and used to communicate with the
people of ancient Israel. During the Graeco-Roman period, that
culture was used for the presentation of the gospel. African
indigenous Christians have taken into consideration African
religio-cultural tradition in presenting the message of God, since
the Bible must be made to speak to the life and thought of the
people in languages and images that are comprehensible to them.
African culture, customs, traditions, arts, metaphors and images
are necessary for Africans to feel at home with the gospel. This is
important because African religio-cultural traditions are closer to
the biblical and ancient Near Eastern culture than the Western
culture, as affirmed by David Garret: 'Africanism is not only good
in itself, but also a culture closer than European to the biblical
way of life, and therefore more suitable for building a Christian
society.'[56]

One important fact that must be mentioned is that the African
indigenous churches in Nigeria, that are using this method, are
growing very quickly compared with the mainline missionary
churches. Ironically, while the authorities of the mainline churches have condemned these indigenous churches for approaching

55. I have discussed earlier the efficacy of the use of water, fasting and
faith in African indigenous culture.

56. David Garret, *Schism and Renewal in Africa* (Oxford: Oxford University
Press, 1968), p. 166.

the Bible this way, many of their members join these churches. In fact, many outstanding church members of the mainline churches prefer to keep their membership intact with the missionary churches, but frequently visit the pastors and prophets of these African indigenous churches. Testimonies of members and non-members who visit these churches either at night or daytime provide powerful evidence of the effectiveness of the use of the Bible this way.

Conclusion

The above shows that the way Western scholars divide the Psalms into various types may not be relevant to African Christianity. The preoccupation with the authorship and dates, the documentary theories, redactionary theories and others, may also not work well for African Christianity. The type of classification in the African context is, of course, based on the actual content of the Psalms, and in addition, on the function and the efficacy of each portion of the Psalter to protect, heal and obtain success in the African context. The justification for the above approaches to the study of Psalms by African indigenous churches in Nigeria is not only effectiveness, but also religio-cultural. The fact is that African Christians do not face the same problems as Western Christians. They need a different hermeneutics that takes cognizance of both their cultural tradition and the Bible.

The above shows that African indigenous Christians are not passive receivers of Christianity. They made use of whatever they learned from the Western missionaries and adapted it to suit their worldview. African indigenous churches have taken greater account of the African worldview and the spirit-world than the missionary churches. They have presented to the world the most indigenous expression of Christianity in Africa. They have made a substantial contribution to the African interpretation of Christian theology through their emphasis on the wholeness of life, community, healing, the reality of spiritual forces, realistic church worship and prayer power.

Admittedly, care must be taken so as not to give the impression that all aspects of African cultural tradition are good. African Christians must be able to sieve what is good and compatible, and throw away whatever is not compatible. This explains the need for the deeper study of African cultural traditions and all aspects of African indigenous churches so that the world can both learn from them and assist in correcting what appears to be wrong. This is an important task that needs to be accomplished. Western Christians, with an abundance of resources and advanced civilization, should contribute whatever they can to develop authentic African Christianity. This contribution may be in the form of assistance in training young people who are ready to do further research in this area of African indigenous culture and Christianity. Further work in this area is urgently needed.

Part II

REINSTATING THE LOCAL

Thinking about Vernacular Hermeneutics Sitting in a Metropolitan Study

R.S. SUGIRTHARAJAH

> I do not want my house to be walled in on all sides and my windows to be stuffed. I want cultures of all lands to be blown about my house as freely as possible. But I refuse to be blown off my feet by any.
>
> M.K. Gandhi

I would like to begin by telling you an urban parable. It is about a peasant and a painter. Actually it is based on an incident that U.R. Anantha Murthy, the Indian writer and critic, witnessed at an academic conference. In fact the painter in the parable was also at the same conference. This painter was narrating his experience of going around villages in North India studying folk art.

Near one of the villages, he was attracted by a lonely cottage at the foot of a hill. Approaching the cottage, he saw through the window a piece of stone which caught his attention. The stone was decorated with *Kumkum*—the red powder that Indian women wear on their foreheads as an auspicious mark. The painter wanted to photograph the stone that the peasant worshipped, and asked if he could take it outside where the light was better. After taking his photograph, the painter felt uneasy for having removed the stone that the peasant had revered and worshipped and expressed his regret. However, he had not been prepared for the peasant's reply, which astonished him: 'It doesn't matter', the peasant told him, 'I will get another stone and anoint it with *kumkum*.' The painter was staggered by the hermeneutical implication of his reply: any piece of stone on which the peasant smeared *kumkum* became God for him. What mattered was his faith, not the stone.

Overwhelmed by the reply, the painter went on to challenge his fellow conference attendees: Did they understand the manner in which the peasant's mind worked? Could they apprehend the essentially mythical and metaphorical imagination which informed his inner life? Was it possible for them to appreciate the complex pattern of ancient Indian thought, since they were all caught up in the narrow confines of Western scientific rationality? Should they not have preferred the so-called superstition of the peasant which helped him see organic connections between the human world and the natural world surrounding him, to the scientific rationality of Western science, which has driven the world into a mess of pollution and ecological imbalance?

The painter persisted. He went on to tell his audience that Western education had alienated all of them utterly from this peasant, and the seventy per cent illiterate Indian mass that populates the Indian villages. In his simplicity, the peasant still kept alive the mode of thinking and perception which had been revealed to the sages from the dawn of time. If they did not understand the structure and mode of this peasant's thinking they could not become true Indian writers. Therefore they should free themselves from the enslaving rationalist modes of Western scientific thinking. Then only would they be able to understand the vital connection between this peasant and his world and between him and his ancestors who had ploughed the same plot of land for generations. Western modes of perception—whether liberal, scientific positivist, or even Marxist—would not enable them to understand what sustained this peasant. These European-born theories, the painter concluded, would only serve to make them feel inferior, and thus turn their country into an imitative copy of the West (Anatha Murthy 1982: 70-73).

Anantha Murthy reports that the instantaneous response of the conference participants was one of embarrassment and shock. They were all profoundly moved by the painter's argument. The painter's peasant stood there before them as an authentic Indian, untouched by the ideas of the grand masters of literary theories, who used the peasant as a mere point of reference to define their positions. The immediate response among the conference attendees was that they had all been alienated from their cultural artistic roots. I will come back to the painter later.

Describing Vernacular Hermeneutics

Recently, Third World biblical scholars have turned their attention to the indigenization of biblical interpretation. Central to the
task is recovery, reoccupation and reinscription of one's culture,
which has been degraded by and effaced from the colonial narratives and mainstream biblical scholarship. What vernacular
hermeneutics tries to do is to erase the painful memory of this
degradation and effacement and to make a fresh start by returning to one's roots. Impelled by a variety of cultural and political
forces, it is an attempt to go 'home'. It is a call to self-awareness,
and aimed at creating an awakening among people to their
indigenous literary, cultural and religious heritage. Etymologically, 'vernacular' connotes the language of household slaves,
hence of ordinary people, rather than that of the masters or the
elite. Vernacular is integral to what anthropologists call nativism.
It favours the indigenous over the exotic. It focuses on cultural
nationalism and self-affirmation in which the colonized, and
others who have been marginalized, seek to vindicate the primacy
of the local over the national and international through the
language, idiom and culture of the common people. It implies a
fierce self-esteem, an assertion of selfhood and self-respect instead
of slavish conformity to received ideas or abject helplessness
regarding one's colonized state. It is undertaken by those who
believe in the values of indigenous resources and those who have
a deep distrust of the centralizing tendencies of Euro-American
critical theories which have failed them. It is a struggle for the
historical and political presence of groups suppressed or
marginalized by colonization and modernization. It is, by
definition, an oppositional category which has come to challenge
the very idea of Eurocentric modernism and internationalism.
Vernacular hermeneutics is not a discrete movement, but part of
the ongoing intellectual and critical movement of our time. It is
postmodern in its renunciation of the Enlightenment meta-narra-
tives and in its elevation of the local as a site of creativity, and it is
postcolonial in its battle against the invasion of foreign and uni-
versalist modes of interpretation:

Nativism, in this sense is an offshoot of the crisis in modernism, a reaction to modernism's alienating aesthetic and its universal claims to knowledge. Nativism, thus, is subaltern—the celebration of the local, the immediate, the marginalised. Hence it is very much a part of the post-modern cultural scenario. There is yet another way of locating nativism. It can be placed in the long and rich tradition of the literature of nationalism and decolonization (Paranjape 1997: 173).

Like any other critical concept, the definition of what is vernacular largely depends on the context. Its meaning is movable and it derives its strength and effectiveness from the opposition against which it is pitted. For instance, during the mediaeval period in Western Europe, when Latin was the language of learning, English was the vernacular. William Shakespeare's works were practically unknown on the continent because they were composed in a language which came third after Latin and French. The Indian situation further illustrates the ambivalence of the term. During British colonial rule with the imposition of first Persian and then English for administration, and the elevation and glorification of Sanskrit by the Orientalists, the recovery of languages like Tamil, Marathi, Bengali and other regional tongues, with their attendant linguistic and belief systems, was regarded as providing an ideal vernacular weapon in the hands of the ordinary people in their clash against the domineering presence of Sanskrit, Persian and English.

Now, however, the situation has changed dramatically and the old dialectical division which used to be invoked in Indian literary circles between the *margi* (Sanskrit) and *deshi* (regional language) does not lend itself to such clear-cut division. The interrelation between the hegemonic Sanskrit and the humble regional languages, or 'vulgar tongues' as the European Orientalists used to call them, is complex and intimate. Indian languages are not self-contained categories. There is much fluidity among them and they continue to interact with one another. For instance, the message of *bhakti*, devotion to God, which was often portrayed as a unique contribution of the vernacular languages of India, was in fact one of the cardinal features of the *Bhagvadgita*, the Sanskritic Scripture which preceded the regional linguistic revival by several centuries. What is more, early converts like Krishna Pillai and Vaman Tilak, although they articulated their new found faith in

Tamil and Marathi, continued to use Sanskrit terms creatively in their writings. Krishna Pillai, for example, utilized phrases such as *sat* (reality), *cit* (consciousness, intelligence), *ananda* (joy) to convey the idea of God. Today, Sanskrit does not wield the power it used to or dominate the Indian linguistic landscape. It is no longer a potential threat as a language. It has assumed, in consequence, the same role as a vernacular language, and Sankritic hermeneutical practices such as *dhvani* (poetic experience), *rasa* (aesthetic relish) and *auchita* (prosperity) are employed by Indians to unsettle the invading foreign critical theories.[1] In such circumstances, Sanskrit is seen as a vernacular corrective to the exegetical protocols set by the metropolitan centres.

Similarly, the imperial role of English has also changed over the years. English in India, in spite of its elitist tone, is seen increasingly as one of the Indian *bhasas* (languages). It played a vital role during the colonial struggle, and continued to coexist with other Indian languages, and contributed to the task of nation-building in the aftermath of independence. English has been successfully nativized by the infusion of indigenous vocabulary which resonates with the ethos of the sub-continent. The distinctive flavour of Indian English comes through vividly in the writings of Salman Rushdie, Arundhati Roy and others. What is more, in a country like India where language is seen as vehicle to whip up communalism, English remains a link and in some ways a unifying force, and is devoid of any communal blemish. So much so that Geeta Dharmarajan sets out to:

> [a]rgue a case for an English that can stand right royally along with the other modern Indian languages—those that are called *bhashas*... Such an English *bhasha* would be its own and yet capture all the immediateness that other languages are capable of (Dharmarajan 1994: 12).

What is vernacular depends on who is using what and against whom. Hence regional *bhashas*, Sanskrit and English can all be used creatively to revise and envision an alternative to invading,

---

1.   For examples of how the Western literary canon has been subjected to these Indian indigenous theories, see Narasimhaiah (ed.) 1994. For the application of these theories in Indian Christian hermeneutics, see *Bible Bhashyam: An Indian Biblical Quarterly* 5.4 (1979) (for the *dhavani* method); and Kampchen 1995 for the *rasa* method of interpretation.

disabling and alienating forces and tendencies.

Vernacular up until now has had only a limited valency in theological circles. Its role has been chiefly to translate books produced in Western languages. What Koyama, the Japanese theologian, who began his career as a theological educator in Thailand, says of that country is generally true of other Third World countries as well:

> In Thai theological education, the function of the vernacular has been largely to explain Western theological words and ideas. The religious images shaped in the Thai spirituality for centuries are either ignored or subordinated to the images imported from the West. The vernacular has lost its own dignity. This goes against the Pentecostal affirmation of every language (1993: 101).

The loss of the vernacular was due to the growing distance of the second and third generations of Indian Christians from their traditional cultures. The early converts, though eventually they drifted away from their own cultures, were organically steeped in them and maintained an organic link with them. The effortless ease with which they delved, with great profit, into their linguistic, regional, cultural and religious idioms, and reworked them into Christian themes, is hardly evident in the current theological literature. Present day Indian interpreters who show competence and acquaintance with Western learning and literature have to make a special effort to employ indigenous themes. The other misfortune is that, because of the civilizing motive of Christian missionaries, Christians have been forced to study indigenous texts in the context of Christian texts. As a result, the greater part of Hindu, Buddhist and Confucian textual traditions have become irrelevant, and the few parts that have become meaningful are due to the forced imposition of Christian/Western categories.

Vernacularization and Biblical Interpretation

What vernacular interpretation seeks to do is to overcome the remoteness and strangeness of these biblical texts by trying to make links across the cultural divides by employing the reader's own cultural resources and social experiences to illuminate the biblical narratives. It is about making hermeneutical sense of texts and concepts imported across time and space by means of one's own indigenous texts and concepts. In opening up the biblical narratives, vernacular reading draws on three key aspects of a culture—ideational (worldviews, values and rules), performative (rituals and roles) and material (language, symbols, food, clothing etc.). In other words, using indigenous beliefs and experiences, cross-cultural hermeneutics attempts to provide important analogies with ancient texts which readers from other cultures may not notice or be aware of. What in effect such readings have done is to make culture an important site for hermeneutics.

Conceptual Correspondences
Surveying the field, one can identify at least three modes of vernacular reading—conceptual correspondences, narratival enrichments and performantial parallels. The first mode—conceptual correspondences—seeks textual or conceptual parallels between biblical texts and the textual or conceptual traditions of one's own culture. Such an attempt, unlike historical criticism, looks beyond the Judaic or Graeco-Roman contexts of the biblical narratives, and seeks corresponding conceptual analogies in the readers' own textual traditions. Indian Christian interpreters of an earlier generation were pioneers in this mode. K.M. Banerjea (1813–1885) demonstrated the remarkable similarities between biblical and *Vedic* texts. He selected overlapping narrative segments touching upon the creation, the fall and the flood from the great wealth of *Vedic* writings, and juxtaposed these with passages from the Bible, emphasizing, however, that the expectations of the Indian texts were fulfilled in Christianity: 'The *Vedas* confirm and illustrate Scripture traditions and Scripture facts. Christianity fills up the vacuum—a most important vacuum—in the *Vedic* account of the sacrifice, by exhibiting the true *Prajapati*—the Lamb slain from the foundations of the World' (Baago 1969: 16).

There are a number of examples of creative borrowing from indigenous concepts. G.S. Vethanayagam (1774–1864) employed the theistic mystical tradition of the *Saiva bhakti* to explicate the death of Christ. Dayanandan Francis, who has done an extensive study of the creative utilization by the Tamil Christians of their own tradition, describes Vethanayagam's ingenious use of *Saiva bhakti* thus:

His attention is focussed on the feet of Jesus. He visualizes his master nailed to the cross. He approaches the feet of Jesus as would a Hindu *bhakta* approach the feet of his Lord. The highest point of mystical union in theistic *Saiva Siddhanta* is the close and intimate contact between the feet of the Lord and the head of the *bhakta*. The feet (*tal*) and the head (*talai*) almost become one while they maintain their distinctive identity. The two words *tal* and *talai* when joined together become *tadalai* according to the grammatical rules of combination. The phrase *tadalai* sounds as one word while it obviously contains two words which have not lost their identity. The union between the *bhakta* and the Lord is similar to this. Vedanayagam longs to experience similar union with the Lord Jesus Christ under whose feet he wishes his head should settle. His longing is that the settlement should be firm and enlivening. So he beseeches that the nails piercing through the feet of Jesus should also pierce through his head. He believes that when this kind of oneness is attained his image will vanish like the iron in the furnace and the image of Christ will enshrine in it. He sings: In order that this wicked one might vanish in your image like a piece of iron burnt in fire/ And that I settle under Thy feet upon the cross so that the nail on Thy feet might pierce through my head (Francis 1995: 118-19).

Dayanandan Francis himself has relocated the Gospels of Mark and John within the Tamil poetic context, and has opened up the magic casements of the Tamil world for Christian readers. His *Vazhvalikkum Vallal* (The One Who Gives Life) (1981) and *Iraivanin Tirumaindar* (God's Holy Son) (1984) weave Tamil aesthetics with the gospel narratives. Another Tamil convert, H.A. Krishna Pillai (1827–1900) compared the practice resorted to by Tamil lovers in the Sankam literature,[2] (where the lover, as an evidence of his love for his beloved, rides, screaming with blood, on a thorny cart made out of a palmyra trunk), to the death of Christ, with his head crowned with thorns, hanging on the cross enduring untold agony (1977: 168). Similarly, A.J. Appasamy (1891–1971) borrowed key ideas from *bhakti*, the Hindu devotional tradition, to make sense of Johannine spirituality. He enlisted concepts like *moksa*/liberation, *antaryamin*/indweller, *avatar*/incarna-

---

2. Tamil bardic and classical literature produced between 300 BCE and 200 CE, regarded as the most creative period of Tamil writing. Sankam means academy, a normative body of poets who adjudicated the worthiness of literary creations.

tion, as a way of getting into the thought world of John. In doing so, he invested these Hindu concepts with Christian meanings and at the same time accentuated the role of Jesus (1928, 1931).

In China, Wu Lei-ch'uan (1870–1944) was engaged in a similar exercise. In his case he was trying to integrate Confucian concepts with biblical concepts. He utilized the Confucian fundamental concept of highest virtue, *jen*, and also *Tien-tzu* (Son of Heaven) and *Sheng Tien-tzu* (Holy Son of God) to elucidate the Holy Spirit and the role of Jesus (see Yieh 1995). The Japanese theologian Kitamori's employment of *tsura* to explain the pain of God (1965: 135-36); the South African artist Mbatha's use of *ubunto* to appropriate the story of Joseph as that not of an individual but of a community; and Gerald West's recovery of the African notions of *indlovukazi* (first wife), *inthandokazi* (favourite wife) and *isancinza* (helper to the wife) as an interpretative key to explain the matrilineal presence and power and to determine the role of Leah, Rachel, Bilhah and Zilpah, in their stories, also fall within this mode (1993: 58).[3]

In this same mode, insights from popular culture are also summoned to illuminate biblical texts critically. Hendricks, the African-American, calls for the use of cultural expressions such as blues, soul and jazz to formulate a guerrilla exegesis (1994). Australian Aboriginals attempt to translate Aboriginal Dreaming stories in to Christian terms, citing passages from both testaments to convey the essential moral message (Pattel-Gray 1995). And the reclamation of two pivotal Indian tribal values, anti-pride and anti-greed, which resonate with the Markan narrative (10.17-27 and 10.35-45) as an alternative model for a world driven by greed and consumerism, are further examples of the utilization of elements from popular culture (Soares-Prabhu 1995).

Narratival Enrichments
The second mode is to re-employ some of the popular folk tales, legends, riddles, plays, proverbs and poems that are part of the common heritage of the people, and place them vividly alongside biblical materials, in order to draw out their hermeneutical implications. C.S. Song, the Taiwanese theologian, who pioneered the method of creatively juxtaposing myths, stories and legends with

3.   See also his article in this volume.

biblical narratives, often went beyond the written word to the symbolic meaning. In *The Tears of Lady Meng*, Song uses a well-known Chinese folk tale and blends it with the biblical theme of Jesus' death and resurrection (1981: 59-66). Peter Lee juxtaposes the book of Ruth and a Chinese drama of the Yuan period, 'The Injustice done to Ton Ngo'. Both stories are about a daughter-in-law and her devotion to her mother-in-law. Both emerge out of a patriarchal society, though they differ in their plots (1989). The ethical and metaphysical perspectives shine through the stories. Samuel Rayan, in his essay, 'Wrestling in the Night', juxtaposes in an imaginative way three texts, two ancient (the *Bhagavadgita* and the book of Job) and one modern, the posthumous writings of a young girl, eponymously entitled the *Poems of Gitanjali*. These three represent three religious traditions—Hindu, Jewish and Islamic. In spite of the time span and different religious orienta-tions, Arjuna, Job and Gitanjali testify that sorrow and pain are universal (Rayan 1989). All three in different ways wrestle with death, pain, love and God, and through sorrow and pain, grow in faith and love. Africans, too, are engaged in retrieving their folk tales. The parable of the Two Brothers, a popular story among the Sukuma people of Tanzania, has interesting parallels with the Lukan Prodigal Son. Both these stories have a father and two sons and in both the younger son is received back into the family and rewarded. Although in their plots and in their thematic emphasis they may differ, the additional insights that the Sukuma parable provides, such as values of community and unity, serve to enrich the biblical story (Healey and Sybertz 1996: 104-106).

Archie Lee engages in a postcolonial intertextual rereading of two poetic traditions, Hebraic and Chinese. He investigates Psalm 78 and the *Book of Poetry (Odes)* or *Shih Ching* and demonstrates how in their retelling these texts privileged a particular royal ideology. One legitimizes the rule of David and Judah, over against that of marginalized Ephraim, and the other elevates the Chou dynasty at the expense of the colonized Shang people: 'These imperial powers have made use of the religious power of the chosenness of God and the threatening concept of the Mandate of Heaven' (1996: 192). In Lee's view it is crucial to listen again to the missing voices like those of Jeremiah and the suppressed Shang, who 'represent the other side of the missing part of the story which at least expresses disagreement' (1996: 193). Lee's contention is that to arrive at a full reality one needs to engage in such a hermeneutics.

Perfomantial Parallels
The third mode is to utilize ritual and behavioural practices which are commonly available in a culture: The Johannine saying of Jesus,

> Very truly, I tell you, unless you eat the flesh of the Son of Man and drink his blood, you have no life in you. Those who eat my flesh and drink my blood have eternal life, I will raise them up on the last day, for my flesh is true food and my blood is true drink (Jn 6.53-55).

may sound awkward and cannibalistic to those who are reared in Western Enlightenment values. But read analogically to Malawian witchcraft talk, as Musopole has done, the saying takes on a different meaning—'anyone who feeds on Jesus takes into themselves the very life-force of Jesus to re-inforce their own lives' (Musopole 1993: 352). Such a reading could be understood metaphorically as a eucharistic saying, or literally as witchcraft talk.

The African concept of trickster, though it differs from context to context, is also a helpful channel through which to appraise the behaviour of some biblical characters, who, viewed from a Western moral perspective, may seem dubious and deceitful. From an African trickster point of view, such actions are recognized as performed by people who lack power and live in hopeless situations. The trickery in question is something men and women often turn to in situations where they have no other recourse. The reason given by Hebrew midwives for their unwillingness to discharge Pharaoh's order to kill all male children born to Israelites (Exod. 1.15-19), Abraham's deceptive statements to Pharaoh and Abimelech (Gen. 12.10-13; 20.1-18), Delilah's attempts to woo and overcome Samson (Judg. 16), Rachel's answer, the 'way of woman is upon me' (Gen. 31.35), as a way of foiling her father-in-law Laban's attempt to verify the truth of whether she has stolen the family gods or not, are examples of the trickster role played in the Bible by individuals who are otherwise powerless (Steinberg 1988).

The importance of olfaction as rites of passage and transition in some African cultures could also open up some of the difficult biblical passages which exegetes, raised up in the Enlightenment mode of thinking, try to expurgate or explain away. One such verse is Isa. 11.3. Modern translations read: 'And his delight shall be in the fear of the Lord.' If translated literally, it would read, 'He shall smell in the Lord'. Such a translation causes uneasiness among cultures which fail to see a potent link between odour and discriminatory powers. God discerns through senses of smell and taste just as much as through the oral and visual. In African traditional religions this is a common practice. In these religions there is a Chief Sniffer, whose role is to sniff every entrant at the worship with a view to check whether the intentions of the worshipper are good or evil. Some African independent churches have instituted the role of a Chief Sniffer. Ian Ritchie who has studied this phenomenon and has been arguing for the democratization of the means of knowing, points out that olfaction in many African religions is 'considered a means of discernment in many respects superior to any other sense, for it can reveal important things not accessible through any other sense'.[4] Because of the disuse of olfactory language among contemporary commentators, there is a reluctance among them to accept the idea of a God or messiah who would discern by a sense of smell. The Hebrew Bible is full of olfactory images, olfactory language and olfactory metaphors of knowledge. The current Western hermeneutical paradigm is heavily biased towards a visual mode of knowledge and equates seeing, especially seeing the text, with knowing. African culture, like Hebrew, is free of this exclusively textualist and visualist paradigm and is in an advantageous position to appreciate the Isaian and similar passages in the Bible.

The Vernacular in Metropolitan Context

The emergence of indigenous ways of reading the Bible by the people of the Third World has given the impression that vernacular hermeneutics is something recent, exotic and confined to the

4.   I rely here on the manuscript form of Ian Ritchie's two articles— 'Bodily Ways of Knowing in the Hebrew Bible: Implications for Biblical Studies' and 'The Nose Knows: Bodily Knowing in Isaiah 11.3'. Though these articles have been accepted for publication, I have been unsuccessful in getting the bibliographical details. My apologies to Ritchie.

cultures 'out there', and that Western readings are devoid of such practices. Biblical interpretation, however, has always been culturally-specific and has always been informed and coloured by reigning cultural values, and Western scholars themselves have not always been entirely free from such tendencies. Even a casual glance at the history of hermeneutics will reveal that there has never been an interpretation that has been without reference to, or dependence on, particular cultural codes, thought-patterns, or the social location of the interpreter. A classic example of an earlier cultural appropriation was, the *Heliand* (Saviour), the ninth-century Saxon epic poem of the life of Christ, in which the four Gospels were re-expressed in Germanic terms, with Christ reimagined as a Germanic chieftain, and the disciples as clan warriors assembled by him as his private army for the battle:

> In its pages Christianity and northern European warrior culture came far closer to a synthesis... This synthesis provided an evangelical basis for the imaging of Christian discipleship in soldierly terms and opened the imagination and the conscience to create the ideal of the northern Christian soldier—the knight. This evangelical synthesis, it might be further argued, even though originally intended as poetic metaphor, facilitated, and was the embodiment of a founding element of the culture of Europe (Murphy 1989: viii).

What the unknown author does with the familiar gospel narratives, such as the infancy narratives, the Sermon the Mount, the Beatitudes, the Lord's Prayer, the Passion and Resurrection, is to accommodate them to suit the prevailing warrior–aristocratic values:

> Its anonymous author envisioned dynamic poetic equivalents so that the impact of the original text, in its Mediterranean cultural context, might be transferred by poetry analogously to a new North-Sea context. Such a task of inculturation had not been undertaken since the evangelists themselves (Murphy 1989: 28).

Another notable example where prevailing cultural codes were summoned to illuminate a difficult biblical concept is the often baffling notion of the death of Christ. Anselm's answer to the problem was to use of the 'analogy of the situation of a mediaeval peasant insulting a king. Reconciliation would not be achieved until satisfaction had been made for the affront to the king's

honour' (Winter 1995: 63). Luther's reinterpretation of justification by faith, which dispensed with a mediator, utilized the then
emerging modernism's core value, individualism. Such mobiliza-
tion of contemporary cultural codes supports Bultmann's claim:
'Every theological exposition of the saving event and the Christian's existence is constructed with contemporary conceptions'
(1969: 279). Bultmann himself utilized Heidegger's existential
philosophy to interpret the New Testament.

A recent example of culture-specific reading in the West was the
work of the Bible and Culture Collective. Uneasy with the interpretative practices which emerged in the wake of modernity, this
group attempted to recover the Bible by subjecting it to postmodern concerns. The introduction to *The Postmodern Bible* reads:

> In reaction, we are arguing for a *transformed* biblical criticism, one
> that would recognize that our cultural context is marked by
> aesthetics, epistemologies, and politics quite different from those
> reigning in eighteenth-and-nineteenth century Europe where
> traditional biblical scholarship is so thoroughly rooted. We are also
> arguing for a *transforming* biblical criticism, one that undertakes to
> understand the ongoing impact of the Bible on culture, and one
> that, therefore, benefits from the rich resources of contemporary
> thought on language, epistemology, method, rhetoric, power,
> reading, as well as the pressing and often contentious political
> questions of 'difference'—gender, race, class, sexuality and, indeed
> religion—which have come to occupy center stage in discourses
> both public and academic. In short, we hope in this volume to con-
> tribute to the process of bringing biblical scholarship into mean-
> ingful and ongoing engagement with political, cultural, and
> epistemological critiques that have emerged 'in modernity's
> wake'…and that have proved so fruitful in other literary studies
> and cultural criticism (The Bible and Culture Collective 1995: 2).

Some Affirming and Constructive Thoughts

With such a breadth of possible readings, one has to admit that
the efficiency and utility of vernacular hermeneutics as a critical
tool is somewhat limited at present. One should not idealize the
indigenous, endow it with redemptive properties, and see it as the
vehicle of deliverance from our entire hermeneutical malaise.
Positively, vernacular hermeneutics has enabled Christian interpreters to gain credibility and cultivate deeper contact with their

own people who otherwise would have regarded Christians as foreigners in their own country. It has also helped to reverse the
missionary condemnation of indigenous cultures. The mobiliza-
tion of cultural insights has also served as an acknowledgment
that religious truths were present in indigenous cultures prior to
the arrival and introduction of Christianity. Even before Vatican II
and the current theology of religions popularized the notion of
positive elements embedded in other faith traditions, earlier interpreters like Banerjea were able to establish this.

Drawing creatively on the indigenous archive, vernacular hermeneutics has played a significant part in rectifying an often one-
sided picture of biblical concepts. For instance, God is often portrayed in male categories. Reaccentuating Saiva and Vaishnavite
concepts of God as male and female, Krishna Pillai and Tilak were
able to rechannel and weave these into Christian discourse.
Marshalling what is explicit in their tradition, they were able to
draw attention to the gaps, omissions and implicit elements in the
biblical narratives The lyrics these men wrote after their conversion demonstrate how the concepts of two traditions intermingle.
Tilak's hymn, still widely used in Indian Christian worship, is a
case in point:

> *Refrain*: Tenderest Mother-Guru mine,
>   Saviour, where is love like Thine?
>
> A cool and never fading shade
> To souls by sin's fierce heat dismayed: (*Refrain*)
>
> Right swiftly at my earliest cry
> He came to save me form the sky. (*Refrain*)
>
> He chose disciples—those who came
> Consumed by true repentance' flame: (*Refrain*)
>
> For me, a sinner, yea, for me
> He hastened to the bitter Tree: (*Refrain*)
>
> And still within me living, too,
> He fills my being through and through. (*Refrain*)
>
> My heart is all one melody–
> 'Hail to Thee, Christ! All hail to Thee! (*Refrain*) (see Jacob
> 1979: 102).

Creatively intermixing and synthesizing biblical faith with
indigenous religion, vernacular hermeneutics has not only trans-

formed the biblical faith. It has also enabled indigenous cultures to survive for instance, Mayan identity in Guatemala.[5] At a time when hermeneutical practices emphasize textual and visual modes as a means to knowledge, vernacular hermeneutics provides a corrective with its emphasis on the non-visual senses, and reverses the bias towards rationalistic understanding, and opens up the richness of non-rationalist modes of interpretation.

What is significant about vernacular hermeneutics is that it did not try to speak to an imaginary or real metropolitan centre. It is evident from the writings of Krishna Pillai, Tilak and others, that the West or the academy did not occupy a central position in their hermeneutical articulations. Certainly they learned and borrowed ideas and techniques from external resources, but they reshaped them, often adding their indigenous texture to meet local needs, and in a few cases they turned their articulations against the European invaders. More importantly, they did not convey their message exclusively through the mode of the dominant thinking. They did not see their task as representing or measuring up to the protocols set by outsiders, but went about their business of redefining imported Christian values to fit the local idiom and ethos. What is remarkable about their literary production was that their audience was an immediate one, and one whose immediate interests they served.

Negatively, in pressing for corresponding cultural elements, vernacular hermeneutics tends to overuse the positive aspects of ancient cultures and, in doing so, is inclined to overlook their dehumanizing aspects. Vernacular hermeneutics does not become automatically virtuous because it draws on native traditions. It can become hegemonic and intolerant of other modes of local communication such as the oral, or of other minority language traditions. The uneasy relationship between Indian dalits and the tribals is a case in point. Indigenous cultures carry along with their enlivening aspects a baggage of feudal, patriarchal and even anti-egalitarian traditions. Vernacular hermeneutics does not gain value because it is expressed in the songs of an *adivasi* (indigenous people) or an illiterate peasant, or found in a few folk-forms and in the writings of modern rural and dalit writers. It is valuable when it celebrates the plurality of the native traditions,

5.   See Hawley: 1996 315-42.

but when it creates an exclusive and a protective past, and in the process silences other voices and hinders the growth of communal harmony, and views contemporary perceptions and attitudes as poisonous, then it has to be challenged. Manipulated by the unscrupulous, vernacularism can degenerate into another form of crude resurgence and an undiscerning glorification of rural and feudal values. Nothing is axiomatically admirable because it is indigenous and local.

The notion that everyone who writes in one of our regional languages and utilizes autochthonous idioms, symbols and ceremonies is always free, emancipated and represents the true India, and that those who write in English and use contemporary western modes of interpretation are by contrast always conniving with Anglo-American or Sanskritic imperialism, is too simplistic. It is tempting to believe that indigenous people have access to privileged knowledge in unravelling the mysteries of ancient texts. To do so would be to reinscribe a hierarchy of hermeneutics in which some have an unequal access and relation to texts. A vernacular writer may actually engage in anti-native cultural practices and turn against his or her own cultural traditions, while a non-native writer in English may actually aid and energize indigenous traditions. The exciting way European missionaries have utilized Sanskritic, Tamil, Bengali and numerous other languages is a case in point. Venacularism can easily degenerate into chauvinism, jingoism or narrow-minded communalism.

Christian vernacular hermeneutics tends to be apologetic and triumphalistic in tone. Since most of the *bhasa* tradition writers were recent converts, they were well qualified to expose the defects of the religion they left behind. Krishna Pillai's *Ratchanya Camaya Nirnayam* (The Determination of the Religion of Salvation) (1898) is an illustration of this. Utilizing his knowledge of the Hindu Scriptures, he constructed his vision of the true image of God, and demonstrated how it fitted in with the biblical notion of God, and went on to expose the failure of his former Hindu deities to measure up to the standard set by their own texts. Nehemiah Goreh (1825–1895) is another who was very severe on his own tradition. Using his profound knowledge of Hindu Scriptures, Goreh was able to refute many of the Hindu claims. In 1860 he published *Shaddarashna Darpa* (literally, Mirror of Six

Systems, i.e. the traditional six systems of Hindu philosophy—
Samkhya, Yoga, Nyaya, Vaiseseka, Minmasa and *Vedanta*). The book,
written in Hindi, was primarily aimed at the Hindu reform
societies of the time, the Arya Samaj and Brahmo Samaj, who
were then engaged in a rejuvenation of Hinduism. The book was
a devastating attack on Hindu philosophical systems and in the
process it demolished the exaggerated claims the European
Orientalists had hitherto made for the ancient wisdom of India,
and also demonstrated that when exposed to reason and logic
these systems were full of inconsistencies and defects. His message
to his erstwhile Hindus was that 'their education in their own
Sastras does not enlighten them' (Gardner 1900: 231).

The other negative feature of vernacular hermeneutics is that it
often makes excessive claims for Christianity and it is prone to triumphalistic tendencies. Thus, the unusual form of altruism *aram*
(the highest form of virtue) which the Tamils claim as their own
inventive property, and which is textualized extensively in their
literature, especially in the Sankam writings, is denied its South-
Indian origin and attributed to Christian influence. Satiasatchy's
contention is that such a supreme form of love, which surpasses
all human standards and defies all religious laws and regulations,
belies its Tamil origin and is more akin to the New Testament
understanding of *agape* and must have come to India with St
Thomas, the Tamils subsequently absorbing it into their lives and
literature:

> Hence we may concede that to Christ's life-style of *agape*, as possi-
> bly introduced by Thomas and as communicated by traders and
> travellers, the Tamil mind has possibly reacted. Consequently, we
> have instances, legendary and historical, recorded in Tamil litera-
> ture from which we have reason to conclude that *agape* in the
> course of time, in some form or other and in varying degrees,
> began operating in the minds and lives of the Tamils (1996: 36).

In making such an assertion, Satiasatchy not only perpetuates the
claim that anything religiously good could only come out of the
Judaeo-Christian tradition, but also denies the possibility that
Tamils could have arrived at this independently. Such claims and
denials alienate the Indian Christian community further from
their neighbours.

The protagonists of vernacular hermeneutics have often used

the argument that interpreters should stick with what they know best, and write about things they are familiar with, and explore their own cultural heritage and drink from their own wells. This way, they argue, one acquires credentials and credibility, and demonstrates one's authentic roots. What such an argument in effect tries to do is to tell the dalits, burakumin, aboriginals, women and the other subalterns that they should deal with and focus on their own territory and not venture beyond their limited space and imagination. The words of the Pulitzer prize-winning author, E. Annie Proulx, are quite apposite here:

> [This] strikes me as the worst possible advice you can give some one, because you are recommending that they not explore life, they do not look beyond their horizons, they not travel or move about, but concentrate on a small scope that is their own internal thoughts and relationships.[6]

Edward Said, too, has expressed his uneasiness about the formation of hermeneutical enclaves: 'I have no patience with the position that "we" should only or mainly be concerned with what is "ours", any more than I can condone reactions to such a view that require Arabs to read Arab books' (1993: xxviii). A contemporary critical practice must retain the right to adapt, adulterate, amalgamate and parody any theories in its struggle to achieve a coherent understanding in a pluralistic world. To cling only to an exclusive single position is to deny other possibilities and options.

Vernacular hermeneutics became a celebratory event when people led a settled life and thought in terms of cultural wholes. But now, at a time when there is an intermixing of cultures, both at popular and elitist levels, and when local/global and vernacular/metropolitan divides are shrinking and peoples' lives are being rearranged by globalization, finding cultural-specific analogues may be an increasingly difficult task; alternatively, of course, the new multi-vision may throw up its own hitherto undiscovered parallels. It is important to see the global/vernacular, rural/metropolitan as relational and relative concepts. To treat vernacular and metropolitan hermeneutics as contrasting pairs—one as narrow, stable, intuitive and closed, and the other as open, progressive, rational and fluid—is to miss the point. The interconnection between the vernacular and the global is now so deep

6.   See her interview in *The Guardian*, 6 June 1997.

that it is very difficult to determine what is native and what is non-native. If vernacular means isolated, excluded and purged of foreign elements, implied narrow-minded communalism, and the whipping up anti-feelings, then it is doomed to fail. A hermeneutics which is capable of distinguishing between local and non-local, and yet achieves continuity and unity between vernacular and metropolitan, is one that is worth upholding and promoting: 'The boundaries of the local need to be kept open (or porous) if the local is to serve as a critical concept' (Dirlik 1996: 42). If vernacularization is held to mean hermeneutically cleansing imported elements extraneous to one's culture, then surely it is bound to be a disaster. But on the other hand, if it means critical freedom to resist cultural imperialism and to challenge dominant ideologies, then it will continue to be an important hermeneutical category.

The threat to the vernacular way of thinking comes not necessarily from the importation of literary theories from outside, but from within. It comes from the rapid social and cultural changes that are taking place within traditional societies. Among other things, it is caused by rapid movement, displacement and resettlement of people due to local wars, environmental disruption and so on. When the preservers and guardians of traditional wisdom and values are uprooted and lose touch with their native knowledge, and their numbers diminish and they begin to disappear being gradually replaced by a generation exposed to and seduced by global values, then the traditional belief system is in real trouble.

Vernacular hermeneutics, like any other textual practice, cannot be a surrogate for real engagement with the everyday business of living. Invoking the native culture and insisting on its purity is less important than real involvement with ongoing life. In an ever-increasingly multi-cultural society like ours, where traditions, histories and texts commingle, interlace and overlap, a quest for unalloyed pure native roots could prove to be dangerous. It could cause complications for the everyday business of simply living with neighbours of diverse cultures, religions and languages. The prime concern for the interpreter must be to facilitate communal harmony rather than to resuscitate a projected, invented or imagined hypothetical identity or a past entombed in a bygone age.

As a way of ending, let us go back to the painter and the peasant. Though Anantha Murthy was moved by the painter's remarks, on reflection, he says that he had a nagging doubt:

> Isn't the authentic Indian peasant, whose imagination is mythical and who relates to nature organically, also an important cult figure of the Western radicals, who are reacting against their materialist civilisation? What if these spiritual reactions in the West are their way of keeping fit, and the 'decline of the West' theory is glibly-repeated humbug?... As a result we keep reacting rather than creating; we advocate the absurd, or in reaction to it admire the authentic Indian peasant—all of them masks to hide our own uncertainties. In the morass of poverty, disease and ugliness of India, isn't the Westernized Indian unauthentic and inconsequential, and the traditional peasant an incongruous and helpless victim of centuries of stagnation? (1982: 72).

Third World theologies, desperately looking for a new mode of perception in the face of new forms colonialism and the threatening features of globalization, are certainly attracted by the simple peasant/aborigine/tribal who has remained through the centuries impervious to the cultures of the conquerors. It is also tempting to freeze a part of the indigene's life as if it represented the whole, and confine him or her to the local. Such an indigene may be no more than a creature of the hermeneutical imagination. Even if that imaginary indigene exists, he or she, like the peasant at the foot of the hill, may not be the least bit interested in the issues discussed here. But as Anantha Murthy says, 'it is important to know that he [or she] exists; our hypersensitive, highly-personal nightmares will at least be tempered with the irony of such knowledge' (1982: 76).

BIBLIOGRAPHY

Anantha Murthy, U.R.
1982   'The Search for an Identity: A Kannada Writer's Viewpoint', in Guy Amirthanayagam (ed.), *Asian and Western Writers in Dialogue: New Cultural Identities* (London: Macmillan): 66-78.
Appasamy, A.J.
1928   *Christianity as Bhakti Marga* (Madras: The Christian Literature Society).
1931   *What is Moksa?* (Madras: The Christian Literature Society).

Baago, Kaj
    1969   *Pioneers of Indigenous Christianity* (Confessing the Faith in India Series, 4; Madras: The Christian Literature Society).

The Bible and Culture Collective
    1995   *The Post Modern Bible* (New Haven: Yale University Press).

Bultmann, Rudolf
    1969   *Faith and Understanding* (London: SCM Press).

Dharmarajan, Geeta
    1994   'Treading Euclid's Line', in Geeta Dharmarajan (ed.), *Katha: Prize Stories Volume 4* (New Delhi: Katha)

Dirlik, Arif
    1996   'The Global in the Local', in Rob Wilson and Wimal Dissanayake (eds.), *Global/Local: Cultural Production and the Transnational Imaginary* (Durham, NC: Duke University Press): 21-45.

Francis, Dayanandan
    1981   *Vazhvalikkum Vallal* (The One who Gives Life) (Madras: The Christian Literature Society).
    1984   *Iraivanin Tirumaindar* (God's Holy Son) (Madras: The Christian Literature Society).
    1995   'Brief Remarks on the Relevance of the Indian Context for Christian Reflection: A Tamil Perspective', in Anand Amaladass (ed.), *Christian Contribution to Indian Philosophy* (Madras: The Christian Literature Society): 113-25.

Gardner, C.E.
    1900   *Life Father Goreh* (London: Longmans, Green & Co).

Hawley, Susan
    1996   'Does God Speak Miskiro? The Bible and Ethnic Identity among the Misteitu of Nicaragua', in Mark G. Brett (ed.), *Ethnicity and the Bible* (Leiden: E.J. Brill): 315-42.

Healy, Joseph, and Sybertz Donald
    1996   *Towards an African Narrative Theology* (Maryknoll, NY: Orbis Books).

Hendricks, Osayande Obery
    1994   'Guerilla Exegesis: A Post Modern Proposal for Insurgent African American Biblical Interpretation', *The Journal for the Interdenominational Theological Center* 22(1): 92-109

Jacob, P.S. (ed.)
    1979   *Experimental Response of N.V. Tilak* (Confessing Faith in India Series, 17; Madras: The Christian Literature Society).

Kanpchen, Martin, and Jyori Sahi
    1995   *The Holy Water: Indian Psalm-Meditations* (Bangalore: Asian Trading Corporation).

Kitamori, Kazoh
    1965   *Theology of the Pain of God* (Richmond, VA: John Knox Press [1958]).

Krishna Pillai H.A.
    1898   *Ratchanya Camaya Nirnayam* (Sivakasi: Chandra Printers).
    1977   *Ratchanya Yathrikam* (Abridged by P.A. Sathia Satchy; Madras: The Christian Literature Society).

Koyama, Kosuke
    1993   'Theological Education: Its Unities and Diversities', *Theological
                  Education Supplement 1* 30: 87-105
Lee, Archie C.C.
    1996   'The Recitation of the Past: A Cross-textual Reading of Ps. 78 and
                  the Odes', *Ching Feng* 39.3: 173-200.
Lee, Peter K.H.
    1989   'Two Stories of Loyalty', *Ching Feng* 32.1: 24-40
Musopole, A.C.
    1993   'Witchcraft Terminology, The Bible, and African Christian
                  Theology: An Exercise in Hermeneutics', *Journal of Religion in Africa*
                  23.4: 347-54
Murphy, Roland G.
    1989   *The Saxon Savior: The Germanic Transformation of the Gospel in the
                  Ninth-Century Heliand* (New York: Oxford University Press).
Narasimhaiah, C.D. (ed.)
    1994   *East-West Poetics at Work* (Delhi: Sahitya Akademi).
Paranjape, Makarand
    1997   'Beyond Nativism: Towards a Contemporary Indian Tradition in
                  Criticism', in Makarand Paranjape (ed.), *Nativism: Essays in Criticism*
                  (Delhi: Sahaitya Akademi): 153-76.
Pattel-Gray, Anne
    1995   'Dreaming: An Aboriginal Interpretation of the Bible', in Daniel
                  Smith-Christopher (ed.), *Text and Experience: Towards a Cultural
                  Exegesis of the Bible* (Sheffield: Sheffield Academic Press): 247-59.
    1995   *The Postmodern Bible* (New Haven: Yale University Press).
Rayan, Samuel
    1989   'Wrestling in the Night', in Marc H. Ellis and Otto Maduro (eds.),
                  The Future of Liberation Theology: Essays in Honor of Gustavo Gutierrez
                  (Maryknoll, NY: Orbis Books): 450-69.
Said, Edward W.
    1993   *Culture and Imperialism* (London: Chatto & Windus).
Satiasatchy, P.A.
    1996   'Theological Exploration into Ancient Tamil Poems', in Joseph
                  Patmury (ed.), *Doing Theology with the Poetic Traditions of India: Focus
                  on Dalit and Tribal Poems* (Bangalore: PTCA/SATHRI): 21-39.
Song, C.S.
    1981   *The Tears of Lady Meng: A Parable of People's Political Theology* (Geneva:
                  World Council of Churches).
Soares-Prabhu, George M.
    1995   'Two Mission Commands: An Interpretation of Matthew 28: 16-20
                  in the Light of Buddist Text', *Biblical Interpretation: A Journal of
                  Contemporary Approaches* 2.3: 264-82.
Steinberg, Naomi
    1988   'Israelite Tricksters, their Analogues and Cross-Cultural Study',
                  Semeia 42: 1-13

Yieh, John Y.H.
1995   'Cultural Reading of the Bible: Some Chinese Cases', in Daniel
            Smith Christopher (ed.),*Text and Experience: Towards a Cultural
            Exegesis of the Bible* (Sheffield: Sheffield Academic Press): 122-53.
West, Gerald
1993   *Contextual Bible Study* (Pietermaritzburg: Cluster Publications).
Winter, Michael
1995   *Problems in Theology: The Atonement* (London: Geoffrey Chapman).

Hermeneutics within a Caribbean Context

GEORGE MULRAIN

Introduction

In this account of 'hermeneutics within a Caribbean context', I propose to identify the underlying techniques which are in operation when the theologians of those islands that are washed by the Caribbean Sea engage in doing biblical hermeneutics. It is important at the outset to appreciate the fact that Caribbean academics do not have the monopoly upon theological activity. This is true of every island whether the main European language spoken is English, Spanish, French or Dutch. In anglophone Caribbean, for example Jamaica, Trinidad and Barbados, although there are colleges which offer biblical and theological programmes of study to persons preparing for the ordained ministry of various Christian churches, there are countless practising theologians whose sole qualification is a love for the Bible and a profound desire to interpret it for their own benefit as well as that of their families and local communities. This latter category includes mothers interested in bringing up their children in the knowledge of God, lay persons exercising leadership roles in their congregations, itinerant preachers yearning to fulfil a prophetic function as they seek to be God's mouthpiece at the roadside, on public transport or in the waiting rooms at clinics and hospitals, indeed those men and women who endeavour to live the Christian faith in their day to day activities.

The manner in which Caribbean persons engage in the hermeneutical process is in keeping with a style that is typical of Black culture. In other words, what we have operating here is an activity that is part and parcel of Black theology. This is no surprise, since a significant percentage of the people in the

Caribbean are descendants of Africans. Before proceeding further, it will be helpful if a brief explanation about Black theology is given, with a view to ensuring that there are no doubts as to its relevance to the Caribbean region. Following this I will go on to outline what hermeneutics within the Black tradition entails—for whom is it done, by whom and for what purpose. This will lead into the meat of what I wish to share, namely to look at preferred hermeneutical techniques within the Caribbean. My hope is that the treatment of this subject will excite some thinking and discussion about the strengths as well as the limitations of Caribbean hermeneutics.

Black Theology in the Caribbean

Black theology is one of the theologies which emerged from the South as a reaction to the manner in which scholars from the North have traditionally done theology. It begins with the premise that theology is contextual, in the sense that it does not emerge in a vacuum but arises out of given contexts. Theology is much more than 'God talk'. It is 'God experience', or the way in which God is perceived by human beings in given situations. There is one God and there are certain aspects of divinity that are constant—immortality, invisibility, omnipotence, omnipresence, omniscience, loving creativity—and as is emphasized within Christianity, the incarnation or self-revelation in Jesus Christ.

It must however be admitted that there is not just one way whereby God is understood by the peoples of the world. God is perceived differently, depending upon who you are and where you are. We are all made differently, hence what makes sense to one individual might be nonsense to another and vice versa. We know this only too well in Caribbean islands where our 'nationals' are from a variety of ethnic backgrounds. The original inhabitants were Amerindian tribes, one of them being the Caribs, hence *Carib*(bean). The invading Europeans brought people from the African continent to work as slaves on the plantations. After emancipation, a serious labour shortage had been created because the Africans refused to go back to the land. A call was therefore made to people from the Indian sub-continent to work as indentured labourers. During this period, namely the latter part of the nineteenth century and into the early part of the twentieth century, significant numbers of Chinese immigrants were added to the region's population. Multi-ethnicity and multi-faith have since then been our lived reality.

Being open to numerous theological insights has been one of our characteristics as a Caribbean people. There are those today, for example, who find it more meaningful to think of God as Mother. The tradition in our region of the world is that women have been more directly involved in the running of the home. As a consequence, the mother or even the grandmother figure communicates more positive images than the father figure. However this truth ought not to negate the fact that persons within the Caribbean have also been brought up by two loving parents and can appreciate and accept any parent image as reflective of God. Persons within this latter category need to be sensitive and humble enough to admit that they do not possess the whole truth when those who have not had their experience and do not share their views challenge them on this point.

The real issue at stake with contextual theologies is how to use limited human experience and limited human forms of communication to speak sensibly about a God who is all-embracing. It is an impossible task. No word has yet been invented to encapsulate God in completeness. No theological system can claim to be meaningful or relevant to every conceivable person on the face of the earth. There is, therefore, no universal, no absolute theology. Black theology is one attempt to present in a way that is most meaningful to people within Black culture—including Africans, African Americans, Black British—the one God who is their God as well as being the God of all the nations. Caribbeans have found quite a lot in this theology with which they can relate.

When persons hear about Black theology for the first time, they tend to question whether one has in effect created a theology that is racist. Racism is about power and the outright refusal of one race to share that power with others. In the Caribbean understanding of Black theology, there is no claim being made that God is for Blacks and Blacks alone; there is no rejection of other theologies. In this context, Black theology is pro-Black without being anti-White. People of other races, nations and cultures are within their rights, just as Black people are, to claim God for themselves and to perceive God in terms that do make sense to them. For the young girl in Africa, if the pictures that are painted of holy men and women, and of Jesus and Mary are White, then it is likely that she will grow up questioning whether she can relate to this God. She will have problems trying to understand God and to appreciate the doctrine of the Incarnation. If God has indeed appeared in the flesh, then why not African flesh? She might also have a problem loving God. Black theology maintains that Black people must love themselves as beings created in God's image and likeness.

> Those who say, 'I love God', and hate their brothers or sisters, are liars; for those who do not love a brother or sister whom they have seen, cannot love God whom they have not seen. The commandment we have from him is this: those who love God must love their brothers and sisters also (1 Jn 4.20-21).

As far as Caribbean theology is concerned, the starting point must also be an acceptance of the culture in which we live and move and have our being.

Black Hermeneutics

What I am saying about different understandings of God applies to the Bible as well. Indeed the Bible is crucial, since this is the book, or collection of books, which contributes towards a disclosure about the nature of God. The fact that there are in existence today several translations of the Bible, and versions within those translations, illustrates that there are differences of interpretation as far as the Biblical message is concerned. This is what hermeneutics is all about—interpretation.

The contention in this essay is that in cultures which espouse Black theology some distinctive interpretations of Scripture have emerged. These will often, though not always, be strikingly different to traditional Western interpretations. To fully appreciate why this is so, we ought to know 'for whom' and 'by whom' the interpretation is given. The hermeneutical exercise within Black culture is not necessarily for the benefit of the academic theologians. It is seen as primarily for the benefit of the masses of people who try desperately to have a faith that is relevant to what they face every day of their lives. In other words, hermeneutics is for the

edification of those persons who constitute the Church. Since
hermeneutics is designed to fulfil an ecclesiological function, it
also follows that those who are best suited to engage in Biblical
interpretation, though not exclusively so, would be the ones who
are sympathetic to the Church's aims and objectives. Fitting easily
into this category will be the preachers who wish to proclaim from
the pulpits in their churches or along the roadside a message
from God, or the Sunday School teachers who want to help the
members of the Junior Church to acknowledge the claims of
Christ upon their young lives. In the Black hermeneutical tradition, therefore, attempts are made to interpret Scripture so that it
helps to nurture in the faith the community of Christ's body.

Some scholars lament this strong link between hermeneutics
and church tradition. They see it as a hindrance, in that there
could be a limitation imposed on the freedom of the interpreter,
who has to be extremely careful that in the interpreting process
there is conformity to church doctrine. Of course, not all scholars
consider this association with the Church to be a bad thing. Cain
Hope Felder, for example, has this to say:

> Even those who regret church influence on academic study readily
> admit that any black interpretation of the Bible must take into very
> serious account the peculiarly intimate link between black biblical
> understanding and the vital life of the black church. Many black
> biblical scholars consider that the black church, far from being a
> liability requiring apology, is in fact one of the greatest contexts for
> black biblical interpretation. The historic witness of the black
> church affords black Bible scholars a rich framework for studying
> the Bible (Felder 1991: 6).

The other thing to be said is that being committed to a particular church tradition does not necessarily rob one of the freedom
to interpret. In actual fact, there is no individual who is so com-
pletely detached from everything as to be rendered one hundred
percent objective. Every interpreter is biased in some way. This is
the very point I am making about the existence of the various
types of biblical hermeneutics. There are Black hermeneutics
because persons who are the products of Black culture will interpret Scriptures in ways that are unique to them and quite different from White interpreters. The other issue to which Black
scholars refer is the 'politics of interpretation' (Felder 1991: 6).
What White European scholars have traditionally offered as *the*

authentic interpretations of texts are in fact Eurocentric interpretations and not universal ones.

There is, therefore, no uniform, unconditional, absolute interpretation. It is a misnomer to speak about universal hermeneutics. The one who interprets tends to bring her or his own bias to bear on the way in which the message is perceived. Just as one person may read a poem or sing a song and in so doing give particular emphases in different places, so it is when a Black person reads Scripture. Certain parts may mean something special and ring chords with what the person has experienced. What that Black sister or brother communicates following what has been read will not be the same message articulated by another person.

Caribbean Hermeneutical Techniques

It was acknowledged above that Caribbean people are a diverse lot, seeing that the region's history is bound up with that of four continents—America, Europe, Africa and Asia. Caribbean theologians have the advantage of selecting from a number of hermeneutical techniques that have been in existence over the years. There is the historical-critical method of the West which tries to find the original meaning of the text: 'What exactly did this passage mean for the people in the context in which it emerged?' There is the concern about literary style, for example the language structure which can reveal important details about a given text. There is the allegorical method which tries to look beyond the literal meaning of the text with a view to discerning some other hidden, spiritual significance: 'What is this passage really saying in a veiled sort of way?'

In helping us to go back to back to the original meaning, the historical-critical method renders a service to Caribbean interpretations. Of course, to focus mainly on historical detail is to produce a rather limited interpretation. The popular procedure in Black hermeneutics is to adopt the approach that there is no textual authority. No text ought to stand unchallenged. A purely Western scientific approach will claim absoluteness in the text, namely that it is fixed, that it emerged in a given historical period, therefore contains an absolute meaning. That may be so, and indeed it is important to be aware of the original meaning and historical context of a text. However, very crucial is the reader's context. Black hermeneutics emerges as a result of the interaction between text and context, particularly the reader's context. The concerns of the interpreter, the problems and questions that are current are crucial. The interpreter looks at the Bible with her or his own eyes and therefore gives particular slants to the interpretation of texts. This means that the text must always be relevant to today's realities and not just those of yesteryear.

In Black culture—and the Caribbean is no exception—when one speaks of the reader's context, it must be realized that it is the 'reader writ large' being referred to. One should read the text from the point of view of the community. Latin American exegetes also follow this method. The communitarian approach is a response to the individualistic approach which Western interpreters delight in. Maybe it is 'safer' to apply the Bible to individual situations. In so doing, you address individual sins and shortcomings and point to the need for individuals to be saved. Once you read it through the eyes of the community or society or nation, then you find yourself radically opposed to and confronting political and economic powers.

If Caribbean hermeneutics is the interaction between the text and the context of the community, what then is this context? First, it is a context that acknowledges that there is more to life than that which is physical. The real world far surpasses what you or I can empirically verify. There is the unseen world which includes spiritual beings, about which mortal men and women are quite ignorant, but about which the Christ is certainly knowledgeable. One therefore finds little reason to question the existence of forces for good and evil. When confronted with Biblical passages which speak of such forces or of angels, of spirits and of demons, there is not the tendency which might obtain in other cultures to demythologize. For example, Paul's reference to 'spiritual rulers, authorities and powers' (1 Cor. 15.24) does not present the Caribbean person with a problem. Jesus' healing of demon-possessed persons (e.g. Mt. 8.28-34) poses no threat to our understanding. When the roadside preacher studies such texts, he concludes that it is his responsibility to convince his hearers that the same Christ who was able to drive out evil spirits has the power to get rid of any demonic forces in people's lives if only they would allow him.

Secondly, it is a context that acknowledges the historical and the lived realities of our people. The experience for Caribbean people has been one of slavery, oppression, colonialism, suffering, victimization, marginalization, anonymity. Hence, when Caribbean people read the Bible, the way they interpret the message will be affected by their knowledge of these situations. They read the Bible as the book which helps to reveal God. As far as they are concerned, the only God who makes sense to them, and whom they can communicate to their sisters and brothers in the faith, is a God who understands what they and their forebears have experienced and who sides with them in their sufferings. They accept that hardships will always feature in their lives. 'Persistent poverty' is the manner in which a Caribbean economist, George Beckford (1983), described the region's characteristics. The islanders know that the climate brings not only warm sunshine and cooling rains, but powerful hurricanes that pay annual visits and wreak havoc and total destruction. Among the most recent catastrophes is that of the small island of Montserrat, adversely affected by intense volcanic activity. Natural disasters do indeed frustrate our attempts to arrive at a stable economic situation. When, in that context, one reads the book of Psalms, one searches for messages of consolation and hope. 'Rest in the Lord. Wait patiently for Him' (Psalm 37.7); 'Though I walk in the valley of the shadow of death, I will fear no evil, for You are with me' (Psalm 23.4).

Thirdly, the Caribbean context is a multi-faith one. Christians are in the majority, but there are significant Hindu and Muslim presences, especially in places like Guyana, Trinidad and Tobago. There are also many whose religious orientation is based on African traditional religion. Biblical stories like that of the Syro-Phoenician woman (Mk 7.24-30) are appreciated for the affirmation which Jesus gives to those who are not Christians. They communicate a message which reminds us that theological insights are not the monopoly of those who are numbered among the body of Christ. Christians tend to don hats of superiority and, therefore, need always to learn how to receive from people of other faiths.

Fourthly, the Caribbean context is one in which liberation is given top priority. There is a preference for texts that deal with liberation from forms of oppression. The Exodus passages in the Old Testament, as well as those dealing with the fight for survival as refugees in Babylon, are particularly meaningful. Caribbean interpreters compare what happened to the ancient Israelites with that which took place when Africans were seized from their homelands and brought to the New World, against their will, to provide labour for the sugar plantations. There is often a parallel made between the Israelites' journey across the desert and the slaves' journey from Africa across the Atlantic. Rastafarians—those belonging to the religious group that deifies the Emperor Haile Selassie 1 of Ethiopia—have preferred passages like Psalm 137, which talk about the experience of being held in captivity and made to endure exile in Babylon. Members of the Rastafarian movement refer to the region's political powers as 'Babylon'. It is for this reason, too, that they consider themselves to be reincarnations of the ancient Israelites.

In the fifth instance, the Caribbean context is dominated by *hope* in the face of suffering. Caribbean people also find meaningful messages in the book of Job. This is noticeable particularly in a country like Haiti, reputed to have been the first Black republic in the New World. Haitians gained their independence from the French in 1804. However, having faced so much political and economic turmoil throughout their history, they, like Job, have had to face disappointment, disillusionment, depression, particularly under the rule of the Duvaliers (1957–1986) and have wondered 'How long, O God, how long will this misery last?' Like Job, they have endured patience under suffering, yet they never reject God. They remain convinced of God's faithfulness and willingness to be their deliverer. 'Bondié bon' (God is good) is an oft-repeated expression in that country. Again, the book of Psalms displays evidence of its resourcefulness for people in the Caribbean region. Psalm 42 is a good example:

> Why are you cast down, O my soul, and why are you disquieted within me? Hope in God; for I shall again praise him, my help and my God (v. 11).

The Caribbean interpreter, as is so true of any other Black interpreter, is a person of faith in God who sees it as her or his responsibility to nurture the faith of those who belong to the community of believers.

In one of his books, James Cone emphasizes that God is on the side of oppressed peoples everywhere. The Scriptures testify to a God who brings about liberation of sufferers. Cone's approach is to see the revelation of God in liberationist terms:

> The hermeneutical principle for an exegesis of the Scriptures is the revelation of God in Christ as the Liberator of the oppressed from social oppression and to political struggle, wherein the poor recognize their fight against poverty and injustice is not only consistent with the gospel but is the gospel of Jesus Christ (quoted in Copher 1993: 72).

The liberation theme is picked up by the African American, Bishop Joseph A. Johnson, Jr. He enumerated four hermeneutical principles (Copher 1993: 71-72):

1. The Christian gospel must be proclaimed in a vernacular of the people and the commentary on Scripture must come out of the Black experience.
2. God is the creator, sustainer, redeemer of the world and humanity and he actively is engaged in the work of liberation.
3. Jesus Christ is the revelation of the power, wisdom and love of God. He is actively engaged in a ministry of healing, liberation and reconciliation.
4. The life, ministry, death and resurrection of Jesus has radically transformed the human situation and has made possible triumphant Christian living.

Johnson's principles seem to strike chords with what Caribbean people will apply as they wrestle with the Scriptures. His first principle is particularly appealing. In Haiti and Jamaica where oral tradition counts for much, the local Creole and patois languages are used to good effect when one wants to be certain that the exposition of the Scriptures is comprehensible to the masses. In addition, one might employ well-known proverbial sayings to illustrate and illuminate the message from the Bible. In this context, therefore, narrative forms are preferable to statements that are couched in philosophical or scientific language. The lesson to be learned is simple—'tell the story' and you are likely to communicate most effectively.

Many modern Caribbean biblical interpreters adopt the approach of seeking out evidence which is mirrored in the text.

This exercise is not dissimilar to what obtains in feminist and womanist theologies. Women are searching for places where they are given noble mention. They are equally taking note of those places where they have not been mentioned but remain invisible. In their investigations they have shown that there are texts which are hostile to the dignity of women. Black womanist theologian Renita Weems has nevertheless seen the overall liberating message of the Bible as acceptable:

> Where the Bible has been able to capture the imagination of African American women, it has been and continues to be able to do so because significant portions speak to the deepest aspirations of oppressed people for freedom, dignity, justice, and vindication. Substantial portions of the Bible describe a world where the oppressed are liberated, the last become first, the humbled are exalted, the despised are preferred, those rejected are welcomed, the long-suffering are rewarded, the dispossessed are repossessed, and the arrogant are prostrated. And these are the passages, for oppressed readers, that stand at the center of the biblical message and, thereby, serve as a vital norm for biblical faith. Therein is a portrait of a God that oppressed readers can believe in (Weems 1991: 70-71).

Weems has some useful insights on how we might interpret some of the biblical material. She encourages Black women to allow the principle of text interacting with context to be the operative rule. Women's experience of suffering can illuminate some of the biblical stories to produce messages that are relevant to today. Following some reflections on the exodus, she writes the following:

> Within that same larger complex of material in the Book of Genesis is the story of the Egyptian woman Hagar and her slave-holding mistress, the Hebrew Sarah (see Gen. 16.1-16; 21.1-21). Here the status, ethnicity, gender, and circumstances of a biblical character have been seen as unmistakably analogous to those of the African American reader. It is a story of the social and economic disparity between women, a disparity that is exacerbated by ethnic backgrounds. It is the story of a slaveholding woman's complicity with her husband in the sexual molestation of a female slave woman. It is a story of the hostility and suspicion that erupt between women over the plight and status of their male sons. It is the story of an enslaved Egyptian single mother who is subjected to the rule of a vindictive and brutal mistress and an acquiescent master.

> ...while the details of Hagar's story offer for the African Ameri-
> can female reader minimal positive strategies for survival, the story,
> by way of a negative example, reminds such a reader what her
> history has repeatedly taught her: *That women, although they share in*
> *the experience of gender oppression, are not* natural *allies in the struggles*
> *against patriarchy and exploitation* (Weems 1991: 75, 76).

The Caribbean interpreter too is engaged passionately in the quest to find Caribbean folk mirrored in the Bible. It has become very important today for theologians to seek out passages with which they can closely identify, maybe because they parallel or are closely identified with the Black experience. What are the passages which highlight the Black presence in Biblical situations? It used to be the suggestion that the only reference to Black people was that of Ham and his descendants who were a cursed race. Some have interpreted this reference as God giving the okay for Black people to be treated as slaves. Ethiopia is nobly mentioned in the book of Psalms (68.31 and 87.4-5), as a symbol of glory, though Copher suggests that there are far more examples of negative remarks made about Egypt, Ethiopia and Black people than positive ones. (1993: 64)

The negative treatment of Blacks in the Bible is also due to a hermeneutical problem. 'Biblical writers were themselves interpreters' (Hoyt 1991: 17). In both the Old and New Testaments, 'writers took traditions and shaped them according to their own contexts' (1991: 18). Paul, for example, dealt with the question of marriage in 1 Corinthians 7 by interpreting what Jesus said in the light of the Corinthian context. We must not assume that the authors of biblical books were pure and unbiased. They had their points of view and understood God in ways that were unique to themselves.

Caribbean interpreters, like others engaged in Black hermeneutics, have to sort out whether passages are negative because the interpreters who wrote them have chosen to be negative. How does one, for example, interpret Song of Songs 1.5? Is the bride saying that she is 'black *but* beautiful' or 'black *and* beautiful'? The preferred conjunction will depend upon the interpreter. Copher cites examples to show that Blacks were not absent from the biblical narratives. Moses got married to a Black, Cushite woman (Num. 12.1). It is interesting to note that the daughters of Jethro, the priest of Midian, described Moses as Egyptian, not as

Hebrew (Exod. 2.19): 'An Egyptian rescued us from the shep-
herds and he even drew the water for us and watered the sheep.'
In the monarchical era, it is mentioned that one of the soldiers in
King David's private army was 'the Cushite' (2 Sam. 18) and that
King Solomon's chief wife was an Egyptian. There is also mention
of the Queen of Sheba exercising sovereignty over parts of Africa
(1 Kgs 10.1-13; 2 Chron. 9.1-12). In the New Testament writings, it
was Simon of Cyrene who helped Jesus to bear the cross. Blacks
identify with the Cyrenian and state that they are the ones who,
willingly or forcedly, are bearing Christ's cross today. It was the
Ethiopian eunuch mentioned in the Acts of the Apostles who
became converted under Philip. Among the congregation at
Antioch were Simeon called Niger and Lucius of Cyrene (Acts
13.1). Copher therefore insists that 'in numerous instances, the
biblical experience is an African experience' (1993: 148). Many of
the young Caribbean men and women who study the Bible are
interested in finding themselves and their situation mirrored in
this much revered book, so as to attach credibility to the Word of
God.

Quite apart from personal presence is the matter of scenic
presence in the Scriptures. It is not difficult for Caribbean persons to see reflections of their own environment in the Bible.
Many of the settings for the ministry of Jesus were rural and
agricultural, hence, it is not a difficult task to understand Jesus'
reference to fields, crops and harvests. The Caribbean person's
familiarity with the phenomenon of absentee landlords makes it
quite easy to understand some of the parables told along similar
lines. So, too, his references to activities in boats on seas and lakes
are very vivid for people whose islands are washed by the
Caribbean Sea.

Caribbean biblical hermeneutics can learn from the different
methods, including the historical-critical and allegorical methods.
However, there are suggestions about techniques that can be
regarded as unique to Black theology. Included in these are
mythology and *imagination*. The fact is that myths play a central part
in the Black tradition. African culture has been known to communicate truths through the oral traditions of folklore. The folk
hero, Anansi, is well known in the Caribbean as one whose
exploits are often related in reference to so many of life's experi-

ences. It is therefore an easy matter for the Caribbean interpreter to capture the sense of a biblical passage whose message is couched in myth. To use the words of Thomas Hoyt:

> If blacks' mythologies and stories have functioned to interpret the Bible, biblical mythologies have also functioned to interpret blacks' story, language, and imagery (Hoyt 1991: 34).

As far as imagination is concerned, this relates particularly to what had been identified initially as the purpose of Black hermeneutics, namely to nurture the faith of the Church. Joseph Johnson, to whom reference was made earlier, had been given some hermeneutical principles by his father (quoted in Felder 1991: 35):

1. Prepare yourself with devotion and prayer prior to your encounter with the Scriptures.
2. Read the entire *chapter* in which the text is located.
3. Become acquainted with all of the stories which lead up to the text and those that follow.
4. What were the problems, the situation of the participants in the story?
5. Read the biblical passages aloud, so as to hear the Scriptures and permit them to speak to you.
6. Discover the human element and the divine element in the situation.
7. You must see what the writer saw, feel what the participants in the story felt, and hear what they heard.
8. Use your imagination and put yourself in the place of the writer and participants of the story.
9. Assume the different roles of the principal characters in the story and act as if you were present when the story was first told.
10. Ask yourself this question, 'What special message does this passage of Scripture bring to your people for their healing and renewal?'
11. Then wait for God to speak.

Hoyt argues that 'if Scripture addresses the whole person, then intellect alone is not enough. The imagination, in conjunction with the intellect, makes it possible for the whole person to be addressed. Images address the person in the concreteness of life, putting one in touch with the senses in a holistic manner' (Hoyt 1991: 37). Hoyt's words ring true for us in the Caribbean. This is why it is acceptable within our region for the barely literate as well as the academic to be given a hearing with regard to the interpretation of Scripture. If we listen only to those who make use of the tried and tested scientific approaches to Bible study, we run the risk of hearing God speak to us and to the people of our region only in limited ways. However, if we remain open to a variety of interpretative voices, we stand a greater chance of capturing the divine message in new and exciting modes.

Conclusion

Caribbean biblical hermeneutics stands in the tradition of Black hermeneutics in that it tends to be selective about what techniques it employs. In being cautious of the historical-critical method and not totally embracing it, Caribbean biblical hermeneutics offers a challenge to textual authority. The text is not everything, but the reader matters. In this approach though, Black biblical hermeneutics in general and Caribbean hermeneutics in particular must be careful lest they end up denying the historicity of facts. However, the new hermeneutical approaches which they propose are to be applauded in that they offer an affirmation of readers' integrity. Sometimes, as a reader of the Bible one may feel belittled especially when one comes up against a difficult text. The fact that *we* matter to God is gratifying.

Perhaps the challenge is for Caribbean biblical hermeneutics to strike a balance lest the reader regard biblical scholarship as not important. This would be unfortunate because scholarship has made and continues to make a valuable contribution towards Christian education. The creative approach is for the two dominant methodologies to exist side by side with each one informing the other. The plural context which is ours in the Caribbean warrants no less.

As far as looking for passages that mirror Caribbean realities or which speak of the theme of liberation, the interpreter will do well to be warned of the danger of proof-texting. Persons who delight in proof-texting will invariably take texts out of context in order to support their own points of view. This is dishonest and therefore hardly likely to be very helpful to members of the community of faith.

Caribbean biblical hermeneutics cannot survive without using the technique of imagination. Hear what Hoyt has to say on this point:

> There are some legitimate cautions to be followed when using the interpretative imagination. One of the more obvious dangers is that a barrage of strange interpretations could result. The church might revert to a kind of subjectivity that would lead to eisegetical fanaticism. In the African American and other traditions, there have always been persons who solely used their imagination, and that to excess. Probably this always will be a problem. One way to curb such occurrences is to interpret images in the manner in which other factors are considered in the historical-critical interpretations of Scripture. Since an image occurs in a context, we have to examine that context before seeking to understand the image (Hoyt 1991: 38).

What Hoyt has said here with regards to the African American context is equally applicable to that of the Caribbean.

As has been the contention in this essay, Caribbean hermeneutics owes much to both Western and Black traditions. It does not reject one approach to the total exclusion of the other. One of its strengths is that it affirms the two major methodological thrusts. It acknowledges that in both systems, there is something of worth to commend itself to Caribbean exegetes. The task of interpreting the Bible for themselves, their families and their communities then becomes a meaningful and exciting adventure.

BIBLIOGRAPHY

George L. Beckford
    1983   *Persistent Poverty* (London: Zed Books).
Copher, Charles B.
    1993   *Black Biblical Studies: Biblical and Theological Issues on the Black Presence in the Bible* (Chicago: Black Light Fellowship).
Felder, Cain Hope (ed.)
    1991   *Stony the Road We Trod: African American Biblical Interpretation* (Minneapolis: Fortress Press).
Hoyt, Thomas
    1991   'Interpreting Biblical Scholarship for the Black Church Tradition', in Cain Hope (ed.) 1991: 17-39.

Sugirtharajah, R.S. (ed.)
    1995   *Voices from the Margin: Interpreting the Bible in the Third World*
                (London: SPCK).
Weems, Renita
    1991   'Reading her Way through the Struggle: African American Women
                and the Bible', in Cain Hope (ed.) 1991: 57-77.
Witvliet, Theo
    1987   *The Way of the Black Messiah: The Hermeneutical Challenge of Black
                Theology as a Theology of Liberation* (London: SCM Press).

The Bible as *Veda*:
Biblical Hermeneutics in Tamil Christianity

M. THOMAS THANGARAJ

Let me begin this essay with some preliminary remarks. The first is about the term 'Tamil Christianity'. Tamil Christianity is a highly complex phenomenon. It is comprised of Roman Catholic and Protestant Christians, whose mother-tongue is Tamil, representing the two major divisions of the Christian Church in Tamilnadu, India. Tamil Protestants include Lutherans, members of the Church of South India, Pentecostals, Seventh Day Adventists and representatives from other denominations. In addition to these complexities, one can consider such factors as the social location of a particular group of Christians, their caste affiliations, the inter-religious settings in which they live, the differences in urban and rural congregational settings, and so on. In view of such diversity, I cannot do full justice in this essay to the question of biblical hermeneutics in Tamil Christianity. What I am presenting here reflects my own perspective as a Tamil Christian theologian and a Protestant belonging to the Church of South India.

Secondly, the *Vedas* (literally, *knowledge, transmitted wisdom*) are the earliest and authoritative Scriptures of the Hindus in India dating from a period prior to 1500 BCE. The *Vedas* contain four distinct sets of writings called *Rig Veda, Sama Veda, Yajur Veda* and *Atharva Veda*. These are collections of hymns, incantations and rules for religious rituals written in Sanskrit. Though the term *Veda* refers strictly to these writings alone, the popular use of the term is less precise. Any religious writing belonging to any period in the history of Hinduism and written in any of the vernacular languages may be referred to as *Veda* by Hindus. Such usage differs from region to region and from language to language. In these instances, the term *Veda* is a metaphorical term for a given 'sacred' writing.

My aim in this essay is to argue that the way Tamil Christians go about interpreting the Bible is shaped, among other things, both by their view of Hindu Scriptures, the *Vedas*, and by their employment of the term *Veda*—the dynamic equivalent for translating the term 'Bible'. This essay will explore the issue at hand in two distinct directions and at two specific levels. The two directions are, first, how Tamil Christians view the *Vedas* and secondly, how Tamil Christians employ the word *Veda* to refer to the Christian Scripture, the Bible. By two levels, I mean the levels of popular Christian piety and of the reflective theological tradition.

Christian Views of *Veda*

First, let me offer a few historical observations. Christianity is believed to have entered the Indian subcontinent during the first century CE. The Orthodox Christians in Kerala claim to come from the line of that tradition. Historians are divided in their evaluation of the evidence for this position, but they agree that by 400 CE there was a strong Orthodox Christian tradition within India and that tradition operated mainly with the Syriac language. As Robin Boyd maintains,

> Although the Syrian Christian community has been culturally closely integrated with Indian society, there has been little or no attempt to work out a theology in Indian terminology... [it] has remained entirely Syrian, based on the Syriac language.[1]

Therefore, it is difficult to unearth the St Thomas tradition's view of the Vedas. The Roman Catholic missions began in full measure with the arrival of Francis Xavier in 1542. His evangelistic work was carried out mostly among the fisherfolk on the western and eastern shores of the Indian peninsula. Robert de Nobili, who arrived in 1605, was among the first to attempt to attract high caste Hindus into the Christian faith. I will discuss his understanding of the *Vedas* a little later in the paper. At this point it is

---

1.   Robin Boyd, *Introduction to Indian Christian Theology* (Madras: The Christian Literature Society, rev. edn, 1975), p. 9.

sufficient to note that the majority of people attracted to the Christian faith by the work of Roman Catholic missionaries belonged to the lower strata within the caste hierarchy.

On 9 July 1706, Bartholomew Ziegenbalg, the first Protestant missionary in India, arrived on the eastern shores of India at Tranquebar near Madras. For the next two centuries, Protestant missionaries from various denominations worked in South India These missionaries also attracted mostly persons from the lower castes to the Christian faith. The fact that both Roman Catholic and Protestant missionaries had won converts largely from lower castes is very pertinent to our discussion here. These were people with no access to the *Vedas*. None of them had read even a single sentence from the *Vedas*. Of course, most of them knew the *Vedas* by name, and it is quite probable that most of them thought of the Tamil Scriptures—both Vaishnavite and Saivite—as the *Vedas*. Yet even those Tamil Scriptures were accessible mostly to only the higher ranks of the Sudra community—the Vellalars and Mudaliars, and in some cases, Nadars—and not to the sub-castes to which most Christians belonged.

The inaccessibility of and ignorance of the *Vedas* contributed greatly to a thoroughly negative attitude among Tamil Christians toward the *Vedas*. This was reinforced by earlier missionary arguments against the truth of the *Vedas*. Some had argued that the *Vedas* were not consistent in their ideas, that they were not understandable to the person in the street, and that the gods they depicted did not measure up to the holiness of God as presented in the Bible.[2] The fact that the Brahmins controlled access to the *Vedas* was also used to question the validity of those texts. These arguments, together with the rhetoric that sets Christian 'revelation' over against all other 'religions', helped form a very negative view of the *Vedas* in popular Christian piety. Therefore, when Christians used the term *Veda* for the Bible, they quite naturally thought of the Bible as the one and only true *Veda* and the Hindu *Vedas* as untrue and, at times, even the work of the devil. I examine the use of *Veda* for the Bible later in this paper.

While popular piety had such a negative view of the *Vedas*, there was a reflective theological tradition in Tamilnadu which

2. For example, see H.M. Scudder, *The Bazaar Book, or Vernacular Preacher's Companion* (Madras: American Mission Press, 1865).

approached them differently. The leading figure in this approach was Robert de Nobili, a Jesuit missionary in the seventeenth century. De Nobili, who studied Sanskrit, was one of the earliest Europeans to have read portions of the *Vedas* in the original language.[3] His writings convey an attitude of respect and fascination for the *Vedas*. Similarly, the first Protestant missionary, Ziegenbalg, also admired the Hindu Scriptures, where he found 'such teachings and passages…which are not only according to human reason but also according to God's word'.[4]

A more interesting and controversial approach to the *Vedas* came from the twentieth-century South Indian Christian theologian P. Chenchiah. He pleaded for the recognition of the Vedas as the Old Testament for Indian Christians. He argued that one could read the Hindu Scriptures in the light of Christ, just as the early Jewish disciples of Jesus had done with the Hebrew Scriptures. The *Vedas*, Chenchiah argued, could prepare a Hindu to recognize, acknowledge and eventually accept Christ. He wrote,

> I can pick up material for an Old Testament in Hinduism making selections in the light of what Jesus said and did. That was exactly what early Christians did and later Hindu converts ought to do.[5]

Most theologians reject this position since it would imply replacing the Old Testament with the *Vedas*; however, it is acknowledged that the Hindu Scriptures can function as what is called *preparatio evangelii*. Brahmabandab Upadhyaya, another Indian Christian theologian, argued for recognizing *Vedanta* as assisting the Christians in their understanding of faith. He wrote,

> We must fall back on the Vedantic method, in formulating the Catholic religion to our countrymen. In fact, the Vedanta must be made to do the same service to the Catholic faith in India as was done by the Greek philosophy in Europe.[6]

Thus, while popular Christian piety viewed the *Vedas* as fallacious, theologians attempted creatively to use the *Vedas* and vedic statements in Christian theological formation.

---

3.   Vincent Cronin, *A Pearl to India: The Life of Roberto de Nobili* (New York: E.P. Dutton, 1969), p. 87.
4.   As quoted by Boyd, *Introduction to Indian Christian Theology*, p. 15.
5.   Boyd, *Introduction to Indian Christian Theology*, p. 158.
6.   Boyd, *Introduction to Indian Christian Theology*, p. 68.

Today, texts from the *Vedas* are used in worship and liturgy, more often by Roman Catholics than by Protestants. For example, the Ashram movement within the Roman Catholic Church in Tamilnadu, led by Fr. Ignatius Irudhayam in Madras and Fr. Bede Griffiths in Trichy, has developed an informed and appreciative use of the vedic utterances in Christian worship. Similarly, Bishop A.J. Appasamy, a Protestant theologian, published a book entitled *Temple Bells*, a collection of prayers, hymns and utterances from the Hindu Scriptures that can be used in Christian worship.[7]

Christian Uses of the Term *Veda*

The use of the term *Veda* for Christian Scripture came to the fore-front in the process of translating the Bible into Indian languages. The translation process was a high priority in the Protestant missionary agenda but not among Roman Catholic missions.

> Though the Roman Catholic missionaries turned certain Biblical passages into Tamil for devotional purposes, to Bible translation as such they devoted little attention; and the Roman Catholic Church had to wait till the middle of the nineteenth century for a Tamil translation of any book of the Bible. The first Roman Catholic version of the New Testament was issued at Pondicherry in 1857.[8]

Roman Catholic missionaries did not spend their time and energy translating the Bible since, as a book, it did not have the kind of primacy for them that it had with the Protestants. Roman Catholics were more concerned with presenting the message of Christianity in their own writings than with translating the Bible. For example, Fr. Thomas Stephens, who arrived in India in 1579 and worked among the Konkani people, wrote a magnificent Marathi poem of 10,962 verses on Biblical history to take the place of the Hindu *puranas*.[9] It is interesting that Stephens saw the Biblical material as *purana* and not as *Veda*. Abbé J.A. Dubois, among others, strongly opposed the idea of translating the Bible

---

7. A.J. Appasamy, *Temple Bells: Readings from Hindu Religious Literature* (Calcutta: Y.M.C.A., 1930).

8. J.S.M. Hooper, *Bible Translation in India, Pakistan and Ceylon* (rev. by W.J. Culshaw; Oxford: Oxford University Press, 2nd rev. edn, 1963), p. 66.

9. Stephen Neill, *A History of Christianity in India: The Beginnings to AD 1707* (Cambridge: Cambridge University Press, 1984), p. 241.

into Indian languages because the translations offered by Protestant missionary societies were of a very low literary quality, and also because the Bible was not easily comprehensible and appealing to Hindus if it was simply translated and given to them.[10] Protestant missionaries undertook similar attempts to that of Stephens. For example, a poetical version of the Bible by Rev. C.C. Macarthur is titled *The Purana of the Holy Word*.[11]

Thus the word *Veda*, in most cases, did not operate as the dynamic equivalent for the Bible in the work of Roman Catholic missionaries. De Nobili used the word *Vetam* (*Veda*) more often to mean *religion, divine utterance, way* or *knowledge*. Of course, he also used *Vetam* to signify the Bible, but not as frequently as he did with the other meanings. Soosai Arokiasamy has done an excellent survey of the ways in which de Nobili used the word *Veda* in his writings.[12] Even today the word *Veda* is used in this sense by those who refer to the Christians as *vedakkarar* (people of the Bible) and the Christian Church as *vedakkovil* (temple of the Bible).

In examination of the Protestant missionary work, it makes very clear that translating the Bible into local languages was one of the highest priorities and that meant one had to seek a dynamic equivalent for the term 'Bible' in this context. Thus *Veda* came to refer to the Bible for those Christians. Before discussing some of the various forms in which the term is used to signify the Bible, I need to mention one point of interest. Since most Christians came from the lower rungs of the caste ladder, their ignorance of and the inaccessibility of the *Vedas* made it easier for them to accept the Bible as the *Veda*. The term *Veda* did not become a bone of theological contention as did the terms for God and Church among others. In other instances, the converts had to substitute a Christian concept, practice or place for the Hindu ones they had before. But they had not had a Veda as such which

10. Abbé J.A. Dubois, *Letters on the State of Christianity in India, etc.* (ed. Sharda Paul; New Delhi: Associated Publishing Press, 1977), pp. 65-68.

11. Rev. C.C. Macarthur, *A Poetical Version in Tamil of the Holy Scriptures*. I. *Genesis and Exodus XX* (Jaffna: Ripley & Strong, 1866).

12. Soosai Arokias-amyh, *Dharma, Hindu and Christian, According to Roberto De Nobili: Analysis of its Meaning and its Use in Hinduism and Christianity* (Documenta Missionalia, 19; Rome: Editrice Pontificia Università Gregoriana, 1986), Chapter 5.

had to be substituted by the Bible. Consequently, it was easy for them to accept the new book as their *Veda*. The study done by C.G. Diehl on the patterns of culture among some Christian groups in South India, and the study by John Carman and P.Y. Luke on the village Christians in Andhra Pradesh clearly indicate how the substitution of *Veda* by the Bible is not at all an issue in the intermingling process of Christian and Hindu cultural values.[13]

Christian poets use the term *Veda* with complete ease and mean by it the Hindu Veda at certain places in their writings and the Bible in other places. Several examples can be given from the writings of Vedanayagam Sastriyar and H.A. Krishna Pillai.[14] These poets use the word *Veda* as interchangeable with *marai*, *aranam*, *agamam* and *suruti*. Therefore, popular Christian piety that was mostly influenced by the Bible and Christian poets saw no problem or conflict with using the word *Veda* for the Bible. In situations of conflict, Christians would say the Bible is *our Veda*, and of course, ours is more true than the Hindus'.

The Tamil name for the Bible has gone through several stages throughout the process of translation. The first translation of the Bible into Tamil by Ziegenbalg bears the title *vedaposttagam* (*Veda* book).[15] The attachment of the word 'book' to *Veda* does help one recognize that this does not refer to the *Veda* of the Hindus. Ziegenbalg did not reserve the word *Veda* for the whole Bible as such. He referred to the Gospels and Acts as *Vedas*, and called them *ancuvedaposttagam* (the Book of the Five *Vedas*). Most often the word *Veda* is coupled with *Satya* (true) to refer to the Bible. For example, the Bible Society in Madras was called *sattiyaveda sangam*.[16] The translation that was published in 1844 had the title

13. C.G. Diehl, *Church and Shrine: Intermingling Patterns of Culture in the Life of Some Christian Groups in South India* (Uppsala, 1965); P.Y. Luke and John Carman, *Village Christians and Hindu Culture: Study of a Rural Church in Andhra Pradesh, South India* (London: Lutterworth, 1968).

14. See Dayanandan Francis, *Christian Poets and Tamil Culture* (Madras: University of Madras Press, 1978). pp. 20, 23.

15. Bror Tiliander, *Christian and Hindu Terminology: A Study in Their Mutual Relations with Special Reference to the Tamil Area* (Uppsala: Almqvist & Wiksell, 1974), pp. 64-69. Tiliander discusses the various ways in which the words *veda* and *agama* are used by the Tamil Christians to refer to the Bible.

16. *The New Testament of our Lord and Saviour Jesus Christ in Tamil* (Madras:

sattiya vetam.[17] Ziegenbalg himself used the phrase *satya vedam* to refer to the Bible. The combination of the terms *Veda* and *agama* happened during the translation of the Bible undertaken from 1858 to 1869 and now called the Bower translation.[18] There the Bible was referred to as *Parisutta Vedagamam* (the holy *Veda-agama*), and this name for the Bible remains among most Protestant Christians even today. Arumuga Navalar, a Saivite scholar from Jaffna who assisted the missionaries in the task of translation, objected to using the word *Veda* for the Bible, claiming that only the four *Vedas* were the *Vedas* and to call any other writing *Vedas* was totally inappropriate.[19] But he was overruled by the committee and the combination of *Veda* and *agama* was seen as a way of distinguishing the Bible from the *Vedas*. This title, *parisutta vedaagamam,* asserted both the holiness of the Bible and its superiority over the *Vedas*: the Bible is a holy book, and it is both *Veda* and *agama* together!

In translating the terms that stood for the Jewish Scriptures within the New Testament, the term *Veda* was used. For example, in 2 Tim. 3.16, we read, 'All Scripture is inspired by God'. Here the word used for 'Scripture' is *Veda vakkiyam* (Bible verse) in the Bower translation. When the Gospel writers refer to the fulfilment of Scripture in the life of Jesus, the word *Veda* appears again.[20] In this context, theology was known as *vedasastiram* (knowledge of the Bible) The Protestant Seminary in Nazareth, South India was called The Tamilnadu Vedasastira Kalluri (College of the Bible).

With the rise of the Dravidian movement in Tamilnadu, the term *Veda* for Tamil came under attack among Christian theolo-

Madras Auxiliary Bible Society and American Bible Society, 1846), title page.

17. *The Holy Bible in Tamil. The Old Testament translated from the original by the Rev. J.P. Fabricius, The New Testament by the Rev. C.T.E. Rhenius and Revised by the Committee of the Madras Auxillary Bible Society with contents of the chapters and chronology, from the English and occasional writings* (Madras: Madras Bible Society, 1844).

18. Hugald Grafe, *History of Christianity in India. IV.2. Tamilnadu in the Nineteenth and Twentieth Centuries* (Bangalore: Church History Association of India, 1990), p. 249.

19. Sarojini Packiamuthu, *Viviliyamum tamilum* (The Bible and Tamil) (Madras: Gurukul Lutheran Theological College and Research Institute, 1990), p. 174.

20. See Jn 19.28, 37; Lk. 24.32; Jn 5.39.

gians. In the meantime, Roman Catholics of the post-Vatican II period emphasized the study of the Bible in congregations and began to use the term *marai* (Scripture) for *Veda*, and the Bible was called *tirumarai* (holy Scripture) or *marainul* (Scripture book). This was not totally new as Fr. Constantine Joseph Beschi, popularly known as Viramamunivar, in the eighteenth century had referred to the Bible as *marai* in his epic poem *Tembavani*.[21] Protestants also followed suit and referred to the Bible as *tirumarai*. This again was not totally new to Tamil Protestants because the site in Nazareth where the seminary was situated was called *Tirumaraiyur* (the town of the tirumarai). When I entered Tamil theological education in the 1970s, Tamil theological teachers were clearly committed to using the term *tirumarai* and never the word *vedam*. This was done, in Tamilnadu, for two reasons. First, *Veda* is a Sanskrit term and we would do well to avoid using it. Secondly, while the Saivites have their *tirumurai*, the word *tirumarai* can be developed in usage as the term for the Bible.

While these changes were going on, the word *viviliyam* has been in usage for the Bible, though not frequently. *Viviliyam* is the direct transliteration of the word *biblion* in Greek from which the word 'Bible' is derived. It is not clear when this particular term came into use. In tracing the history of the translation of the Bible into Tamil, Kulandran simply mentions that the word *viviliyam* comes from the Greek term 'biblion'.[22] However, it is clear that the term 'viviliyam' was in vogue during the nineteenth century itself. In objecting to the use of the term *Veda* for the Bible, Arumuga Navalar uses the term *viviliyam* for the Bible.[23] In recent years, 'viviliyam' has come to the forefront, this time for different reasons. *Vedas* do refer to the Hindu *Vedas* and, therefore, if one respects the integrity of the Hindu religious tradition, one should refrain from using *Veda* for the Bible. However, *tirumarai*, while meeting the demands of a pure Tamil term for the Bible, does

21. *Veeramamunivar iyattiya tempavani (curukkam)* (commentary by V. Maria Anthony; Tuticorin; Tamil Ilakkiya Kalagam, 1960), p. 4.

22. Sabapathy Kulandran, *Kiristava Tamil Vedagamattin varalaru* (The History of Christian Tamil Vedagamam) (Madras: The Christian Literature Society, 1967), p. 2.

23. Sarojini Packiamuthu, *Viviliyam*, p. 174.

not meet theological demands. *Marai* means 'hidden', and that is not a theologically appropriate term for the Bible, which is based on revelation. Thus, Christian theologians in Tamilnadu today prefer the term *viviliyam* instead of *Veda* or *Tirumarai*. The most recent translation of the Bible—the interconfessional translation undertaken by jointly by Roman Catholics and Protestants in Tamilnadu—bears the title *tiruviviliyam*.[24] This use of *viviliyam* fits well with the growing concern among biblical scholars in India to engage in Biblical hermeneutics in a multi-scriptural context. In this situation, one needs to affirm the particularity of each scripture, and using the word *viviliyam* affirms the uniqueness of Christian Scriptures while respecting the integrity of the Hindu scriptural tradition. This concern and the desire to use pure Tamil words come together in this most recent term *tiruviviliyam*.

If this trend continues, then there will be a need to find a dynamic equivalent for the term 'Scripture' within the Indian setting. In my opinion, the use of *Sruti* to denote Scripture may find more acceptance among theologians than the term *Veda*. Christian theologians in India have all along discussed the *pramanas* (lit. rule or standard of authority) of Christian theology with words like *sruti* (lit. heard), *smrti* (lit. remembered), *anubhava* (lit. experience) and *yukti* (lit. reason, inference). Bishop A.J. Appasamy, in his book *What Shall We Believe?: A Study of Christian Pramanas*, discusses the Bible in four chapters under the heading *Sruti pramana*.[25] If Tamil Christian theologians find *Sruti* to be a problem because it is a Sanskrit term, they may opt for *urai* (lit. utterance, word) within the Tamil Saivite *alavaiiyal* (lit. measure) as the more appropriate term to refer to the Scriptures.

What I have outlined so far exhibits a clear movement away from the devaluation or the co-option of the term *Veda* to a deep respect for the integrity of *Veda* as denoting the primary Hindu Scripture. This movement from devaluation to deep respect has serious implications for biblical hermeneutics in Tamilnadu. Let me mention a few. First, it helps the process of historicization of

24. *Tiruviviliyam (Tindivanam)* (India: Tamil Nadu Biblical Catechetical & Liturgical Centre, 1995).

25. Madras: The Christian Literature Society, 1971. See also Robin Boyd, *Khristadvaita: A Theology for India* (Madras: The Christian Literature Society, 1977), Chapter 2.

the Bible. The Bible as *viviliyam* is placed alongside *Veda* with its own distinctive history and development. Such a placement helps one to recognize the historical in the process of hermeneutics. Secondly, biblical hermeneutics can enter into an enriching and extremely helpful dialogue with the vedic methods of interpretation of sacred texts once the integrity and distinctiveness of each scriptural tradition is forthrightly acknowledged. Conversation becomes the overriding ethos of biblical hermeneutics and not competition or confrontation.

INDEXES

INDEX OF REFERENCES

INDEX OF AUTHORS